Raymond Gudas

Gerbils

Second Edition

Everything about Purchase, Care, Nutrition,
Diseases, Breeding, and Behavior

With 33 Color Photographs
Illustrations by Michele Earle-Bridges

Consulting Editor: Matthew M. Vriends, Ph.D.

BARRON'S

© Copyright 1995, 1986 by Barron's Educational Series, Inc.

All inquiries should be addressed to:
Barron's Educational Series, Inc.
250 Wireless Boulevard
Hauppauge, New York 11788

International Standard Book No. 0-8120-9020-9

Library of Congress Catalog Card No. 94-46721

Library of Congress Cataloging-in-Publication Data
Gudas, Raymond.
    Gerbils : everything about purchase, care, nutrition, disease, breeding, and behavior / Raymond Gudas ; illustrations by Michele Earle-Bridges. — 2nd ed.
        p.   cm.
    Includes bibliographical references (p.   ) and index.
    ISBN 0-8120-9020-9
    1. Gerbils as pets. I. Earle-Bridges, Michele. II. Title
SF459.G4G83 1995
636′.93233–dc20
                                94-46721
                                      CIP

Printed in Hong Kong

6789   9955   987654

Important Note
This book deals with the keeping and care of gerbils as pets. In working with these animals you may occasionally sustain minor scratches or bites. Should this occur, have the wounds treated by a doctor at once.

Photo Credits
Dick Hamer: pages 48, 53, 62; Gräfe and Unzer: pages 4, 12, 58, 59; Aaron Norman: front cover, inside front cover, pages 8, 9, 16, 17, 24–25, 29, 45, 66, 67, inside back cover, back cover; Judith Strom: pages 13, 21, 32, 37, 40, 41, 49.

About the Author
Raymond Gudas, former editor of *Pet Age* magazine, is the author of Barron's *Doberman Pinschers.*

Contents

Preface

Early one morning as I sat in my living room, lazily meditating over a cup of coffee, I suddenly detected something from the corner of my eye—a tiny, floating black spot on the floor near the kitchen doorway. I immediately turned my head to investigate, but saw nothing out of the ordinary. All was quiet and still.

I hadn't been awake very long and was tempted to attribute this apparent hallucination to my still lingering drowsiness. But I remained suspicious, so I trained my eyes on the floor and waited. Seconds later, near the foot of the doorway, the black spot, which I now recognized to be a small mouse, reappeared. After sniffing around for a few seconds, the animal vanished again, somewhere behind the refrigerator.

Most people, upon making such a sighting in their home, typically react with some combination of annoyance, fear, and disgust. For me, it was different. As the former editor of *Pet Age* magazine, the country's largest pet industry trade publication, I routinely edited articles on a variety of creatures—large and small. So perhaps it was unavoidable that my interest in all kinds of animals has come to exceed the bounds of normalcy.

Besides, through the years I have happily shared my home with an assortment of pets—including many gerbils. And so, strange as it may seem, I felt a certain fascination with even this, the gerbil's rodent cousin.

I couldn't help it. Despite definite differences, gerbils and mice do have similarities, among them living environments, breeding activity, certain food preferences, and, of course, the trademark of all rodents—incisors that grow continually throughout their lives.

Don't get me wrong. I realized full and well the absurdity of my initial reaction to my uninvited houseguest; but at the same time, it served to remind me how understanding the physiology and behavior of an animal—any animal—inevitably increases our appreciation and enjoyment of it.

Not coincidentally, that happens to be the ultimate purpose of this book. By understanding the origins and characteristics of gerbils, their housing and health needs, as well as proper handling, breeding habits and general behavioral traits, it is hoped that the gerbil owner will be able to provide the best possible care and establish the best possible relationship with his or her pet.

If this book has met that goal, it will not have done so by words alone. It is therefore only fitting that I express my sincerest thanks to photographer Aaron Norman and artist Michelle Earle-Bridges, whose work adorns and enlivens these pages. I should also like to thank my friend and mentor Matthew Vriends, Ph.D., who patiently guided me through this project; Fredric L. Frye, D.V.M., whose suggestions are incorporated in this new edition; as well as the staff at Barron's for their continuous encouragement and support. This book represents the results of all our efforts.

One last detail remains—the mouse in my kitchen. A neighbor insists I'll have to set a trap for it, but I'm still hoping I'll be able to talk it into submission.

Raymond Gudas

Origins and Characteristics of Gerbils

Gerbils in General

It's not surprising that most people—even those who consider themselves well versed in zoology—know little or nothing about the remarkable creatures known collectively as gerbils.

Unlikely as it may seem, most gerbil species were not even discovered until this century. As human empires and armies came and went across the globe, these quiet, unassuming but intelligent little animals went about their daily tasks of survival largely

Most gerbil species were not discovered until this very century. As man's empires and armies came and went across the globe, the animals went about their daily business without much notice.

unnoticed, save by the foxes, snakes, and birds of prey into whose food chain they happened to stumble. On the infrequent occasions when a human being came across a gerbil in the wild, more often than not it was mistaken for one of its relatives the mouse or the squirrel.

Order: Rodentia

A good guess, actually. Gerbils belong to the scientific order that taxonomists have dubbed Rodentia; this means, yes, that they are rodents, but that shouldn't be held against them. Besides mice and squirrels, so are gophers, woodchucks, guinea pigs, and porcupines—some 40 percent of all mammals, as a matter of fact.

In purely physical terms, rodents represent a rather diverse cast of characters. What they all have in common, however, and what justifies their placement into a single biological category, is that, unlike the rest of the animal kingdom, their incisor teeth (the ones in front that are used for cutting) grow continually throughout their lives.

Frequent gnawing—the rodent's trademark and favorite pastime—keeps the incisor teeth manageably short by continually scraping away enamel (the hard, glossy outer layer of teeth). Otherwise, they would continue growing until they resembled tusks, eventually piercing the animal's mouth.

Gerbils, like all rodents, have front teeth that never stop growing. So if you have a gerbil pet, be sure to give it something to gnaw on.

This gnawing activity, though necessary for the rodent's well-being, has always been a source of anxiety for human populations in their midst, and for this reason many rodents have acquired a bad reputation. People forget, however, that even rodents serve a purpose in the total scheme of things. They destroy weeds and harmful insects; they have proved useful in laboratory experiments; they provide a source (sometimes the only source) of food for other animals, as mentioned earlier, and also for human beings in some parts of the world; and certain varieties, such as the beaver, the chinchilla, the muskrat, and the so-called great gerbil of Russia, like it or not, continue to provide highly prized fur.

To further differentiate the large grouping of animals broadly defined as rodents—many of them seemingly totally unrelated, aside from their dental makeup—taxonomists divided the order Rodentia into 33 families, with each family consisting of at least one genus (plural: genera) and species.

Family: Cricetidae

Gerbils, to be specific, belong to the family Cricetidae. Within this family, however, there are several genera of rodents that are commonly known as gerbils, with each separate genus made up of a prescribed number of species. For example, the Mongolian gerbil, by far the most popular gerbil available today, is a member of the genus *Meriones,* of which there are a dozen individual species. The so-called pygmy gerbil, on the other hand, is one of 54 species belonging to the genus *Gerbillus.*

Gerbils vary in size from 2 to 9 inches (5–22.5 cm), the tail accounting for close to half the length. Covered with hair and ending in a bushy tip, the tail serves a dual purpose. The appendage helps support the animal when it stands up to survey its surroundings and also acts as a kind of stabilizer when the animal leaps through the air—an often used means of locomotion among desert rodents. Other outstanding features are the broad, elongated head; the large nose and eyes; the rounded, high-set ears; the long, kangaroo-like hind legs; and the rather short forefeet, with paws that function much like hands. Anger and excitement are expressed by a rapid drumming motion with the long hind legs. Gerbils are astonishingly fast movers, capable of outrunning even a cat!

The bulging eyes—black in most cases; occasionally brown—provide excellent vision, a trait the gerbil does not share with very many of its rodent relatives. It also has an acute sense of hearing, attributed more to the enlarged, sound-amplifying cavities *(tympanic bullae)* in its skull than to the ears themselves, which are not particularly large.

Fur color varies to a certain extent. Typically, it ranges from soft brown to reddish brown, although shades of gray and even yellow are not uncommon. Often, thick black hairs are interspersed throughout the coat. Beneath this outer layer is a denser undercoating of smoky gray fur. Belly fur is

Frequent gnawing—the gerbil's trademark and favorite pastime—keeps incisor teeth manageably short by scraping away enamel.

The whiskers of a gerbil work as sensing tools. With them gerbils can discern temperature changes, rough and smooth surfaces, and breezes.

usually white, sometimes cream-colored or light gray. The dark outer coat helps camouflage the animal if it ventures out before nightfall; the always lighter underside serves to reflect the desert heat of its native habitat, protecting the vital organs from dehydration.

In its entirety, the Cricetidae family contains more than a hundred genera. These include muskrats, lemmings, pygmy mice *(Baiomys taylori)*, Peruvian puna mice *(Punomys taylori)*, and lesser known varieties, such as aquatic rats and Central American water mice. As a group, their range is worldwide, though the gerbils among them are found only in the sandy regions of Africa, Asia, and parts of Europe—more specifically, Turkey, northern Africa, the Middle East, the Caucasus region of the Soviet Union, southwest Asia (including India and Sri Lanka), Mongolia, and northern China.

Gerbils in the Wild

Burrows: In the wild, gerbils live in underground burrows—passageways

excavated in the sand. This arrangement provides the best protection both from predators and from the scorching rays of the sun. Many gerbil species are, in fact, nocturnal, rarely if ever venturing outside during daylight. This fact may help to explain why their contacts with human beings have generally been so few.

Burrows, which are often several feet deep, may simply consist of a single tunnel, or may include several small rooms connected by passageways. Except for a few notable exceptions— the Mongolian gerbil, for example—gerbils are not especially sociable animals. More often than not, in species that live in family units (not all do), each burrow in a community is home only to members of the same family, and outsiders are not tolerated. Fighting often results when a stranger appears.

Food is scarce in the desert regions where most gerbils dwell, but they adapted long ago to these conditions, making do quite well with what is available to them, including

In the wild, gerbils normally obtain sufficient water from the plants that they consume.

seeds, stalks, tubers, roots, and flowers. Some species are known to store food in their burrows—this makes perfect sense considering the harsh and unpredictable nature of their environment—but this behavior is not apparent with gerbils in captivity. A few species have cheek pouches, either external or internal, which greatly facilitate the food-gathering process.

Water, normally obtained in sufficient amounts from the plants the gerbil consumes, is stored in the body in the form of fat. When water is not available from common, everyday sources, the animal can draw on these reserves to keep it alive until new sources can be found.

Hibernation: Under extreme conditions, many species hibernate, but not at the same time of year. Depending on the local climate, some gerbils do so only during the winter months, when it becomes unbearably cold; others only during the summer, when oppressive heat makes activity intolerable.

Reproduction: As mentioned earlier, not all species live in family groups. The so-called Jerusalem gerbil, for example, prefers—in fact, demands—to lead a solitary existence, aggressively delivering this message to any other gerbil that might assume otherwise (except during mating season, after which it invariably returns to its "bachelor" ways). Libyan and Mongolian gerbils, on the other hand, take mates for life; and if one of the pair dies, the survivor is not likely to accept a new partner.

Most female gerbils come into heat every five to ten days. The typical gestation period is three and a half to four weeks, the result of which may be a litter of anywhere from one to ten (the average is four to five) pups, as newborns are called. Breeding activity varies considerably in that some species will have half a dozen litters each year, whereas others will restrict themselves to only one.

Hardly more than 1 inch (2.5 cm) long, babies arrive into the world

Gerbils can maintain an energetic pace when they reawake because they rest or sleep frequently throughout the day. In cold weather they like to huddle close to their cage mates.

toothless, blind, deaf, and lacking even a trace of fur. As you might imagine, the first few days are critical to their survival. They develop quickly, however, if proper nutrition is provided, and by the end of two weeks will already be covered with a light coat of hair. A few days later, they will have their incisor teeth. Weaning occurs sometime between the twenty-first and twenty-eighth day.

By the time they are three months old, gerbils are sexually mature. There is little visible difference between males and females, but careful observation reveals that the latter are usually a bit smaller. Also, the female's underside tends to be rounded, with the anus and vagina positioned close together. The male's rump is somewhat tapered, and the genital area is surrounded by a distinct patch of dark gray hair.

As soon as they mature, gerbils leave the burrow to find mates and establish homes of their own. If this biological timetable appears to be a fast one—as indeed it does, compared to our own—consider that a gerbil's lifespan is only a scant five years. And note that this figure is derived from

gerbils in captivity; those in the wild are less likely to live as long.

Activity and rest: The gerbil's daily routine is characterized by intermittent periods of intense activity—be it burrowing, tending to young, or foraging for food—followed by short periods of sleep. The cycle is fairly constant, such that gerbils do not seem to sleep much overall. When they do, however, they snuggle up close to each other for comfort. This habit is retained in captivity, and two or more sleeping gerbils are an amusing and endearing sight.

The Mongolian Gerbil

Admired for its inquisitive nature (one might say it is downright nosy) and its receptiveness to human beings, the Mongolian gerbil *(Meriones unguiculatus)* easily leads the pack in general availability and in pet store sales.

Discovered by a French scientist in the early 1950s, Mongolian gerbils were soon captive-bred by Japanese researchers, who in 1954 made some of the offspring available to their American counterparts. Found to be an ideal candidate for laboratory research, the Mongolian gerbil soon became recognized as an equally fine pet. Today, more than ever, this friendly animal is finding a place in pet lovers' homes and hearts.

Morphology

In terms of physical characteristics, the Mongolian gerbil basically fits the norm. A typical adult measures approximately 8 inches (20 cm) in length (including the tail), its total weight averaging 4 ounces (approximately 113 g). Fur coloring tends to be of the reddish brown variety, with lighter-colored hair circling the eyes and highlighting the ears. As with most species, the underside is white.

The gerbil's body is somewhat stocky, a characteristic that becomes

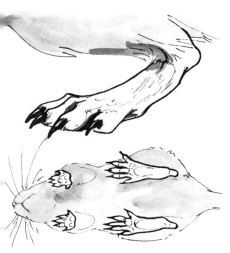

Gerbils' hind paws have elongated toes and fairly long, jet-black claws. They enable gerbils to stand firmly, even on the constantly shifting sands of the desert.

most apparent when the animal squats on its powerful hind legs to scan the horizon, as it does frequently when moving about. Although the tail does its part to help steady the animal in this position, the brunt of the effort is borne by the extra-long hind feet. Each foot has five toes, which comprise almost half the length of each foot. Aside from having the same jet-black nails (or claws), the hind feet are not at all like the front paws, which may have four digits each (sometimes the "thumbs" are absent) and are noticeably shorter.

Behavior

What the forelegs lack in size, they more than make up for in dexterity. The handlike paws are extremely efficient for digging, and they handle food with almost acrobatic skill, much like the paws of squirrels, which Mongolian gerbils resemble to a degree.

The similarity does not end with the paws. Like squirrels, the Mongolian gerbil moves on all fours, making the same kind of quick stop-and-go movements as it proceeds on its rounds. It is capable of making rather impressive (for its size) leaps—as much as 1½ feet (45 cm), horizontally—but does not normally travel this way. Nevertheless, leap it will if it is startled. This is why the animal is sometimes referred to as the "kangaroo rat."

In the wild, the Mongolian gerbil has no specific mating season, as many other animals do. If conditions are right, it will breed practically anytime, except during the winter, producing as many as six litters per year.

Gerbils as Pets

Gerbils—specifically, the Mongolian gerbil, but also the rarer and lesser known Egyptian gerbil—make wonderful pets, in terms of both relatively simple maintenance requirements and, more importantly, owner satisfaction.

On the maintenance side of the equation, they take up little space and don't generally mind confinement; they do not smell (unlike mice), are clean, and produce minimal amounts of

Gerbils' handlike front paws are extremely efficient for digging, and they handle food with almost acrobatic skill.

When you take an animal as a pet, you are initiating a relationship in which a living creature will be reliant upon you for its survival. It is a commitment that implies very definite responsibilities, the least of which is providing food and a place to sleep.

waste; they have simple (and inexpensive) feeding requirements; and they tend to enjoy and maintain good health. These friendly animals can be kept in any room that is free from drafts or strong sunlight, but is not too dark.

As for owner satisfaction, here too gerbils rank high. In behavior and appearance (just look at that face!), they are unique, displaying qualities that are a constant source of delight. Because they are highly intelligent, gerbils are able to develop recognizable individual traits. Most amusing, however, is the intense curiosity they tend to display toward their surroundings. When it comes to exploring their environment and the elements that compose it, gerbils are downright fearless, sniffing and evaluating practically every square inch. They never sit still for very long.

For all of these reasons, gerbils make especially good pets for children. Not only do they provide a valuable introduction to the pleasures and duties of responsible pet ownership; they also open a young person's eyes and mind to the wonders and workings of the entire animal kingdom.

Once your gerbil knows you well, you can pick it up, but make sure you handle it carefully.

Unfortunately, there are areas where gerbils are not permitted as pets. At this writing, the California and New Mexico Fish and Game authorities prohibit ownership of the animals throughout their jurisdictions.

Purchasing A Gerbil

Considerations Before Purchase

An amazing, and truly sad, statistic in this and other "civilized" societies is the large number of animals that are abandoned—most often to gruesome ends—by their owners on any given day. One tends to think first of dogs and cats (they roam the streets, and animal shelters are bursting with them), but the list includes every kind of pet: reptiles, fish, birds, and even animals that were captured in the wild and could never have been transformed into pets.

Responsibilities of Ownership

People who should have never taken responsibility for an animal, who bought it on a whim or for some other inappropriate reason, grow tired of their charge. They then simply toss the creature, which more than likely has grown completely dependent upon them, out of their lives without a thought for the consequences.

All of us can righteously condemn the heartless individual who dumps a defenseless animal out onto a deserted road in the middle of the night, but what about those of us who have our pets destroyed, or who abandon them to equally irresponsible strangers or to already overcrowded shelters, for the wrong reasons—because the animal is sick or getting old, because we're tired of taking care of it, or maybe because we're moving and it's inconvenient to take the animal with us.

Certainly there are legitimate circumstances when, for one reason or another, one's relationship with an animal doesn't work out. Perhaps it is too aggressive or destructive, or perhaps a child in the family develops a severe allergy toward the pet. All too often, however, people are guilty of failing to consider the responsibilities of pet ownership from the very beginning.

When you take an animal as a pet, you are initiating a relationship in which a living creature will be reliant upon you for its survival. It is a commitment that implies very definite responsibilities, the least of which is providing food and a place to sleep.

More specifically, in regard to these two basic responsibilities, you have to ask yourself these questions: Are you willing to make sure that the animal is fed *properly*, every day, with the right kind of food? Will you provide it with a comfortable, *sanitary* environment, which, in the case of gerbils, means regular and thorough cleanings and changes of bedding material? Your pet's health will certainly depend on these two necessities.

Beyond that, will you actively involve yourself with your pet, taking the time to observe its health, to give it attention, to play with it, and, yes, to communicate your affection? What is a "pet," after all, but a playmate, a companion? Certainly it is not some kind of decoration or conversation piece for the home. You have to be willing to invest a certain amount of effort to fully enjoy and appreciate the animal and to bring your relationship with it to its full potential.

Pets for Children

For parents who are considering buying gerbils for their children, all of this means making sure that the youngsters are indeed ready and willing to take on a pet. It probably also means getting involved themselves, helping to supervise the animal's care and seeing to it that feeding and cleaning schedules are routinely maintained. It's important that *everyone* understands and accepts what is required to keep the animal healthy and happy.

Where to Buy and What to Look For

Choosing a Pet Store

The best place to buy gerbils is a well-run pet store. You might save a little money by going to a breeder, if you can find one; but since gerbils cost little to begin with, it hardly seems worth the effort. Besides, you'll still have to go to a pet shop to buy food, bedding material, a water bottle, perhaps a cage or aquarium to keep the animals in, and whatever toys and other supplies you'll need. You can do everything in one trip.

Children should be included, of course—but not simply because they'll have fun running around the store, as all kids do. If the pet will be entirely theirs, or even if they'll only be sharing in the responsibility for its care, it's wise to have them involved from the outset.

You'll know you've picked a good pet store if it gives the impression of being clean, orderly, and well stocked, and, most important of all, if the salesperson who assists you seems knowledgeable and is willing to spend some time with you. This is certainly the time to ask questions, as many as you can think of.

One, Two, or More?

The first thing to consider, after you've decided what particular species you prefer (there will probably be several to choose from), is how many gerbils you want. More often than not, gerbils are purchased in pairs. Even though some species do prefer a life of solitude, the ones available as pets belong to the more sociable varieties; they prefer companionship. This is *not* to say that you can't keep a single gerbil as a pet, but if you do, it's even more important to give it regular attention.

If you decide to start with a pair, you'll have to determine whether you want two males, two females, or one of each. If you have an interest in breeding, the choice is obvious, but note that a male should be housed only with one female. If you do not wish to breed, some experts say that two females are best, because males are more likely to fight with each other. A pair of females, on the other hand, can be quite happy together (it's endearing to watch them groom each other).

A mature gerbil tends to fight any other gerbil it has not been paired with, so choose your pets from the

Two gerbils from different litters must be introduced to each other gradually or they are likely to fight. Allowing the animals to sniff each other—under careful supervision—is one way to get them used to each other's scent.

Gerbils provide a valuable introduction to the pleasures and duties of responsible pet ownership. They also open a young person's eyes to the wonders and workings of the animal kingdom.

same batch, or deal with a pet shop that keeps the animals in pairs. If somehow you should end up with two strangers, you can try to get them acquainted, but you'll have to do so gradually, housing them separately until they no longer fear each other. You can start by placing them in each other's cages for a while every day. This will get them used to each other's scent. After perhaps a week, hold one (carefully!) in each hand and allow them to sniff each other. Do this daily for at least another week; then try placing them in the same cage. Observe them for a while until you are satisfied that they accept each other.

Before selecting the particular gerbil you want, find out how old the various animals are and inquire about the breeder. To ensure the best chance of

a successful relationship, you want to start out with an animal that is healthy and normal in every way. Just as you wouldn't want to take an ill animal, neither do you want one that is temperamental, skittish, or belligerent because it was mistreated by its former guardian.

Some prospective owners prefer a pair that has just been weaned, that is, removed from dependency on their mother's milk. This is usually accomplished by the third week of life. Young gerbils are a lot easier to train, for one thing, and age is an important consideration if you intend to breed the animals. Other than that, it's perfectly all right to buy gerbils that are as much as several months old, although pairs should be selected from the same group. In fact, some experts say that it's preferable to buy gerbils after

they've already lived together for a considerable time, because there then can be little doubt that they have accepted one another.

Choosing Your Gerbil(s)

Observe the animals for a while before you actually begin the selection process. Even if the entire crew is asleep, your presence should enliven them very shortly. Their sense of curiosity will demand that they investigate the giant face peering down at them, and this is the perfect opportunity for you to make your own observations.

If for some reason a group remains lethargic, it's quite possible that illness is present, so move on to another group. Certainly something is wrong if they don't react to you—healthy gerbils simply don't sit still for very long.

By the same token, eliminate from consideration any individual animals that do not seem alert and responsive.

In selecting the animals you intend to adopt, start by examining the coat. As with other animals, fur is an excellent indicator of a gerbil's general health. It should be shiny, thick, and smooth, with no bald spots anywhere. Neither should there be any sores or cuts on the body, the tail included. If the tail does have cuts, they are often the result of fighting. They'll heal, but pass on the animal anyway, or you could end up with a troublemaker in your home. Should part of the tail be missing probably the result of some unfortunate accident—the gerbil is likely to be normal in most other respects, but why would you want to pay for damaged goods?

Taming your gerbil is a matter of gaining its trust. The way to do this is through frequent contact with the animal, allowing it to become familiar with your scent.

Continuing the inspection, make sure that eyes are clean and bright, showing no sign of secretion or foreign matter, which may signal a cold or other, more serious problems. Also check that the anus isn't smeared with droppings, as diarrhea is another likely sign of illness. Finally, you might also try to observe the animal's breathing, but do not attempt to pick it up to do so, especially if you are not familiar with the proper procedure. For one thing, you can easily hurt the animal, or you may frighten it, prompting it to bite you. In either event, the animal will have had a negative reaction to you; and, because it will remember your scent, this can get an otherwise promising relationship off to a bad start. Save the introductions for when you get home; there's a proper way to go about them, which will be discussed later.

Even if, in the selection process, you managed to pick a gerbil up without encountering any difficulty, consider that human contact, particularly with a stranger, is bound to put the animal into a state of some excitement, flawing any attempt at honest assessment. Instead, study the animal in a non-stress situation. Labored or noisy breathing is the danger sign to look for.

My Tip: Your last chance to discover potential shortcomings before you buy comes after you've announced your choices to the salesperson. Watch how the animals react as they are removed from the cage. If they try to bite, or appear excessively nervous, feel free to voice your concern and ask to see a different pair.

Costs: Purchase and Maintenance

Fortunately, money is not a significant factor where gerbils are concerned, as they are quite inexpensive, averaging only $5 or $10 apiece. Your biggest expense will be the cage or aquarium to keep them in. Expect to pay $20 to $45 for a decent one, more if you decide to get elaborate housing.

It's all downhill from there. Toys and accessories won't cost more than a few dollars each, with the exception of a water bottle, which is priced just a little higher. You can expect to pay about $4 a month (per gerbil) for food, even less if you give them some of your own fruit and vegetable scraps.

Subsequent chapters will deal with specific aspects of gerbil maintenance. For now, let it suffice to say that the gerbil, in spite of its small size and its characteristically friendly nature, is actually a rather hardy animal. For centuries it has survived—in fact, thrived—in some of the most inhospitable climates on the planet. To that extent, it is capable of withstanding quite well even what might be described as major changes in its environment. These include the confinement and temporary discomfort of the trip home, not to mention the additional adjustments involved after it gets there.

The Trip Home

The salesperson at the pet store should he able to provide you with a suitable container in which to carry your gerbils home. Of course, if you buy a cage or aquarium at the same time, you can simply carry the animals inside.

In either case, if you'll be traveling a considerable distance, provide bedding for the animals. Since sawdust or wood shavings can get a bit messy as a cage is moved around, a better short-term solution is shredded tissue paper. It isn't necessary to provide food or water for a short trip; probably the animals will not want to eat while they're being transported, and water is too easily spilled. On the other hand, it's not a bad idea to place a few carrots or other root crops inside the container, just in case.

If you already have a suitable cage or aquarium at home and will therefore transport the animals in the makeshift container the salesperson gives you, do yourself and your new pets a favor by making sure the permanent home is as ready as you can make it in advance. The smoother the transition from store to home, the less anxiety the animals will have to endure. If, on the other hand, you have purchased a new cage or aquarium, place the gerbils in a sturdy box out of harm's way while you set up their permanent living quarters.

Be careful when transferring gerbils from one container or cage to another. It's wise to place both on the floor or a table, so that if you lose control of one of the animals—either because it panics or because you didn't handle it properly—it won't suffer a serious fall. Probably the safest way to make the transfer is to place the carrying cage inside the permanent one (or up against its open door) and let the gerbils find their own way out.

An animal will experience a certain amount of stress when it faces a major change in its environment. Keeping

If you already have a suitable cage at home (and will, therefore, bring the animals back in the makeshift container the sales-person gives you), make sure the perma-nent home is as ready as you can make it in advance.

that in mind, after establishing your gerbils in their new home, find a quiet place for the cage and, having supplied them with sufficient food and water, leave them alone for a day or two. This will calm them down and help them adjust to their new surroundings.

Housing

Space Requirements

Before proceeding to the specifics of housing, a word of advice may be in order. Some experts recommend a minimum of 36 square inches (approximately 232 sq cm) of living space for each gerbil in captivity; others insist this isn't nearly enough room. One thing is certain: gerbils are highly active animals, so the more room you provide them, the better. A cramped environment is likely to lead to aggressive behavior. It will also hinder—and in all likelihood prevent entirely—the animals' normal breeding activity, assuming that you have a breeding pair and this is your desired goal.

Even if it is not, there is a more important reason to provide each gerbil with as spacious a living area as is

You can provide several opportunities for diversion if you put a small nesting box in a corner of the cage. Not only will the animals have a "cave" to hide or relax in, you can also fashion a ramp, giving them access to the roof. If you leave enough room between the walls of the shelter and the sides of the cage, your pets will have a tunnel-like passageway to enjoy as well.

reasonably possible—that is, the animal's happiness and well-being. An animal confined to an inadequate or barely adequate living space will not live as long as one that has room to move about, to climb and explore and otherwise amuse itself with whatever diversions and activities are available. Similarly, neither will it be as interesting or enjoyable a pet.

In short, the amount of living space you provide will determine whether the animal's environment will be its prison or its home. How often you let your gerbil have the run of the house (carefully supervised, of course) has little or no bearing on the situation.

Types of Housing: Cages and Aquariums

Many different types of *cages* are suitable for housing gerbils. These are highly adaptable creatures, so it really doesn't matter which type you choose. The primary consideration is that the cage be escapeproof and that it provide easy access for feeding and cleaning.

Most of the cages available commercially are made of plastic, metal, or wood. Each of these materials has specific benefits, but each has certain drawbacks as well.

Plastic cages, for example, are lightweight and easy to clean. They also hold heat well; this is important since gerbils, like virtually all other mammals, are susceptible to colds and other ailments of the respiratory tract. The drawback to plastic cages is that they are rather easily gnawed— the gerbil's favorite pastime. This disadvantage is not simply a matter of aesthetics; plastics can be toxic to the

There are a wide variety of ready-made gerbil homes available at your local pet shop.

Before you buy a gerbil home, think about the work involved in cleaning it. If you decide on a home with plastic toys, be sure it has no sharp exposed edges your pet can gnaw on.

You may notice gerbils chewing on cage bars from time to time. This is not unusual behavior, and no harm is likely to come of it. The animals are simply indulging their natural nibbling instinct.

animal. If you choose a cage made of this type of material, make sure that all exposed edges are covered, preferably with metal.

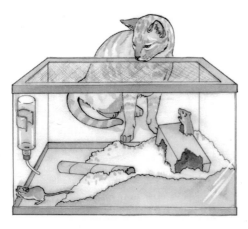

Keeping an aquarium-type cage covered with wire mesh is important, not only to keep gerbils in, but also to prevent other animals from having access to them. Cats are probably the greatest threat.

All-metal cages are chewproof, of course, but they don't retain heat very well, and they have the added and inevitable drawback of contracting rust. They are also heavier than other types of cages. Heat retention is not a problem it the cage is kept in a temperature-controlled environment. Rust, however, is a real concern, since particular areas of the cage (usually the corners) will serve as the gerbil's bathroom. Gerbil urine is highly acidic, thereby facilitating the rusting process. Rusted areas can always be painted, but be sure to use nontoxic and lead-free varieties of paint, such as the type recommended for children's furniture.

Wood is the "natural" choice, perhaps, in that it exudes a certain warmth, both real and imagined, that is lacking in most manufactured materials. Unfortunately, it is also absorbent and therefore requires more fastidious attention when it comes to cleaning. It is also particularly susceptible to gnawing, so, as with plastic cages, its exposed edges should be covered with metal.

Cages come in a great variety of designs—from simple rectangular units to multilevel models and even complex multiunit arrangements connected by series of tunnels. Most can (and should) be easily disassembled for cleaning.

If you fancy yourself a handyman, you might decide to build your own cage. Wood is the logical choice; and if you happen to find an old drawer of suitable dimensions, all you need do is apply a roof and whatever finishing touches may be required.

Another common type of gerbil housing is the simple *aquarium*. Its chief advantage is that it offers maximum visibility, at the same time providing complete protection from drafts. The lack of air flow, especially in smaller aquariums, can become a problem, however, as the resulting buildup of moisture will collect on the floor dressing, requiring it to be changed more often. To maximize evaporation, a wire-mesh cover should be used.

My Tip: Even if the walls are high enough—12 inches (30 cm) or better—that escape is impossible, it's not advisable to leave an aquarium completely uncovered. This is especially true if you have a cat in the house in which case you had better batten down the hatches!

Types of Bedding

Like cages, bedding is a matter of personal preference.

Sawdust is the popular choice; it is inexpensive, abundant, and, most important, rather highly absorbent. Coarse softwood is by far the best, as it is soft, warm, and thick enough not to crumble readily—the chief complaint against fine softwood and pine sawdust. As the latter varieties deteriorate, they form a fine powder that can seriously irritate the gerbil's nose and eyes.

Wood shavings: Alternatives to sawdust—all of which have certain disadvantages—include wood shavings (such as pine and aspen, although not as soft); specially treated or scented commercial substitutes (considerably more expensive); sand (cold and poorly absorbent); newspaper (unclean and potentially toxic); and peat (unclean and powdery when dry).

Gerbils are tidy animals by nature, but the floor dressing will nevertheless have to be changed with some frequency. Soiled areas should be removed at least every two or three days under the best of circumstances, and a complete change of bedding should be provided at least once a week, more often if the cage is on the small side (or has several tenants). Don't wait until the cage smells; ideally, it should never reach that state.

Porcelain food and water dishes are by far the best utensils. Plastic ones are easily gnawed—and plastic can be toxic to the gerbils.

Food and Water Dishes

Containers for food and water should be fairly sturdy—porcelain is a good choice—and the weight and design should be such that the dishes cannot readily be overturned.

The best way to provide a clean source of drinking water is to install an automatic water dispenser, which you

Food and water dishes should be fairly sturdy and of sufficient weight and width so that they cannot be overturned easily.

Today, more than ever, the gerbil is finding a place in pet owner's homes and hearts.

Keeping water in an open bowl is bothersome, because gerbils inevitably get it filled with floor dressing as they dig and burrow in the cage. Frequent water changes become necessary.

The best way to provide a clean source of drinking water is to install an automatic water dispenser, which you can find in any pet store. Gerbils prefer to obtain water from the foods they eat, but drinking water should always be available anyway.

can find in any pet store. They are not expensive and provide a continual source of water. However, you must make sure that the end of the tube does not touch the floor of the cage, or the water will drain away. Note, however, that gerbils rarely partake of water directly, preferring instead to obtain it from the fruits and vegetables they eat. Nevertheless, a source of water should always be available.

Be certain to wash and sanitize thoroughly the entire watering device at least once weekly to prevent an accumulation of bacteria introduced each time the gerbils drink. This can be done with hot water and a weak bleach solution. Be certain to rinse the bottle, rubber stopper, and sipping tube thoroughly to remove any traces of the chlorine bleach.

Nesting Material

Though not absolutely necessary, it's a good idea to provide gerbils, even those of the same sex, with a nest box in a corner of the cage. As burrowing animals, they will enjoy the privacy it provides—be it for sleeping or for sheltering newborn pups. The size depends on the species, but make sure the box has a roof that opens easily for cleaning and inspection, and an entrance large enough to accommodate a pregnant female.

The alternative to a nest box is to provide the animals with an abundance of bedding material, in which case they will gladly fashion their own nest. Almost any soft material can be used for this purpose, although hay and burlap are generally considered the best. As for the latter choice, don't concern yourself with the task of shredding it—gerbils are well equipped to do it themselves.

Almost any type of cloth, as long as it is colorfast, can be substituted for burlap. The exceptions are wool and wool blends, which can block the intestine if swallowed.

Whatever type of bedding material you provide, be sure to change it frequently—preferably, with every regular cleaning.

Toys and Other Diversions

As mentioned earlier, gerbils are most content when they have sufficient diversions available to keep them occupied. Most pet stores carry all kinds of inexpensive toys suitable for gerbils—ladders, balls, bells, mirrors, and so on—and most bird toys will also be happily accepted.

You can also find plenty of appropriate playthings by scrounging around the house. Items to look for include toilet paper tubes, thread bobbins, and tiny cardboard boxes—just about anything, as long as it's not made of potentially toxic or otherwise dangerous materials. Keep in mind that any items you put in the cage will be gnawed until they are barely recognizable, for that is the gerbil's trademark.

Another welcome diversion is a small sandbox (or an amply sized bowl filled with sand). Gerbils like "bathing" in the substance, which you can buy from any construction company or hardware store. Avoid sand from natural sources, as it is likely to

Most pet stores carry all kinds of inexpensive toys suitable for gerbils—ladders, balls, bells, mirrors, and so on. Even bird toys will usually be happily accepted. You can also find plenty of appropriate playthings just by looking around the house.

contain dirt and abrasive elements that can harm the animal.

Caution: Finally, if you're tempted to buy your pet a hamster wheel—*don't!* Gerbils can be seriously injured on such devices, the typical result being amputation of the tail. The newer type of wheel—constructed of solid plastic—appear to be much safer than the ones made of metal wire.

Food

Nutritional Requirements

All living things need a combination of foods to grow and maintain life—that is, to provide the energy needed to fuel muscular activity and basic bodily processes, such as tissue development, heartbeat, and breathing.

From a scientific standpoint, not a great deal is known about the specific dietary requirements of gerbils, mainly because they only recently became the object of human interest.

This is not to say that you, as a gerbil owner, are in the dark when it comes to providing a complete and balanced diet for these animals. Trial and error and common sense have prevailed over time, providing one with a substantially clear picture of what is required to keep your charges in the peak of health.

Gerbils in the wild have to make do with whatever is available to them—primarily seeds, but also grain, grass, certain insects, stalks, and roots. As you have already learned, they do quite well, even on a limited menu. In captivity, the diet you can provide is infinitely more varied. What is crucial, for your purpose, is that the animals get the *right* mixture of all the important nutrients they need: proteins, carbohydrates, fats, minerals, and vitamins.

Animals use *proteins* to build tissues and to spur the biochemical processes that take place in them. For example, collagen, a common structural protein, is the stuff of which muscle tendons are made. Another structural protein, keratin, occurs in the hair and claws. Proteins also supply the main component of enzymes, the catalysts that speed up biochemical reactions, not to mention antibodies.

Carbohydrates, made from small molecules called sugars (or saccharides), promote heat and energy within the body. They also comprise a broad range of so-called polymeric substances (having the same chemical composition, but different molecular weights and properties), such as starch and cellulose.

Fats are used by animals to store energy and to shield them from the cold. Almost as common as carbohydrates, they also serve as "insulators" for nerve fibers.

A diet composed solely of proteins, carbohydrates, and fats is not enough to keep animals (or people) healthy. A wide range of organic compounds, better known as minerals and vitamins, is essential to a balanced diet, although many are needed in only minute amounts.

Minerals are found in a broad range of food materials and serve many functions. Those supplying iron, for example, help oxygen exchange in the body; calcium and phosphorus, together with magnesium, are components of bone; iodine is needed for control of metabolism; potassium is important in nerve and muscle function; fluorine is good for teeth. Other essential minerals include sulfur, zinc, copper, chlorine, sodium, and manganese.

Vitamins occur naturally in many foods, but they are also manufactured by the body. Vitamin A prevents night blindness and various skin disorders; vitamin B_1, affects the nervous system,

Gerbils need salt, so attach a mineral spool to the side of their cage, or place it in a holder (see drawing) in their home.

If anything is difficult about feeding gerbils, it is deciding which of many food alternatives to provide and determining how much of each is enough.

You will soon realize that your gerbil's nutritional requirements can be easily satisfied. They will eat just about anything you give them.

29

circulation, and the gastrointestinal tract; vitamin B_2 affects the skin and eyes; vitamin B_6, important in metabolism, also affects the nervous system; vitamin B_{12} is needed for DNA synthesis and for maturation of red blood cells; vitamin C (ascorbic acid) prevents scurvy; vitamin D is essential for normal growth of teeth and bones; vitamin E is important in reproduction, muscle development, protection of red blood cells, and many other biological processes; vitamin H protects fur from discoloration and hair loss, and it also affects the mobility of limbs; vitamin K is vital for blood coagulation.

Providing a balanced diet ensures that all of your pet's nutritional needs will be met. The best way to do this is to think in terms of variety, which is what a balanced diet is all about. Even though you don't know the *specific* dietary requirements of gerbils, by thoroughly covering the nutritional spectrum—in other words, providing a little bit of everything (with a few restrictions, of course)—you can make sure that all of the requirements will be satisfied.

A varied menu is also kindness. No living thing, human being or beast, can remain satisfied with the same diet day after day. Have you ever noticed the dog and cat owners who buy a case or more of a single type of canned food at one time? Pity their poor animals! This is more than a display of ignorance; it qualifies as reckless behavior as far as their pets' well-being is concerned. Lack of food variety often leads to apathy, loss of appetite, irritability—even illness. Keep that in mind, and vary your pet's diet from time to time.

Types of Food

If anything is difficult about feeding gerbils, it is deciding which of the many food alternatives to provide and determining how much of each is enough.

Liquid multi-vitamin drops should be added to your gerbil's water to insure it gets all the essential vitamins it needs.

Other than that, the job is an easy one, because gerbils are quite easily satisfied—in fact, they'll eat just about anything you give them. Unfortunately, that includes some foods that, for one reason or another, aren't good for them and others that should be given only in moderate amounts. That's why it's so important for you to learn to manage diets effectively.

Premixed Food

A good basis for a gerbil's diet is the special premixed assortments available in pet shops. Often, these are designated as both hamster and gerbil food, as the animals have similar nutritional requirements. The mixtures typically contain sunflower and assorted birdseeds, corn, oats, wheat, and other foodstuffs. Contents vary among different manufacturers, so read the labels carefully for nutritional information; while you're at it, check the milling dates.

Gerbils eat a great variety of foods, including hamster-type pellets, sunflower and other seeds, peanuts, and corn. The only difficulty about maintaining a suitable diet, is deciding which of the many alternatives to provide and determining how much of each is enough.

You can save money by buying these mixtures in bulk, but that means setting up an effective (clean, dry, and verminproof) storage container. A metal one, with a tightfitting lid, is best.

Pellets

An alternative to premixed diets is the pellet foods made for rabbits, mice, hamsters, rats, and other small animals. Most of these will supply a balanced diet, but read the label and make sure the protein content is at least 20 percent. Because the pellets are hard, they have to be gnawed to be eaten, thereby providing the added benefit of helping to file down the gerbil's incisor teeth. The drawback, even if the brand you choose is nutritionally complete, is that the pellets mask the flavors of the individual foods contained in them. Animals are likely to tire of these foods after a while, especially if they constitute all or most of their diet. Note also that young gerbils may have difficulty gnawing on these pellets, which often match them in size; in this case, break the pellets into more manageable pieces.

Preparing Your Own Mixture

Some gerbil owners prefer to make their own food mixtures. These typically consist of some combination of the same foods found in the premixed packages (oats, corn, wheat, seeds, etc.), with any number of additions and substitutions (wheat germ, millet, buckwheat, sugarless cereals, food pellets, peanuts, etc.).

The above may seem like an incredible quantity of food, until you consider that a typical adult gerbil will require only a tablespoon or so of this mixture per day (more for pregnant or nursing females; less for young gerbils). Let experience be your guide—you can afford to, because gerbils rarely overeat. With that said, a few qualifications are in order.

Fruits, vegetables, and even certain wild plants are much enjoyed by gerbils. These foods are important for their valuable vitamin and mineral content, although excessive amounts can have negative effects.

Sunflower seeds: The first area of caution concerns sunflower seeds, one of the few foods gerbils will overeat, usually with gusto. Most gerbils are crazy about them—to the extent that many will eat almost nothing else if the seeds are available. Of course, this means that the overall nutritional spectrum you are trying to maintain would be destroyed. Unfortunately, that's not the half of it.

Sunflower seeds are very high in fat, and gerbils that overconsume these tasty, innocent-looking seeds are flirting with obesity, which in turn can lead to numerous health problems. For females, obesity can hinder breeding (fat often blocks off the ovaries); for both sexes, it can cause respiratory and circulatory ailments, much as it does in human beings. For these reasons, it is best to provide sunflower seeds somewhat sparingly. Keep in mind, however, that obesity is the culprit, not sunflower seeds per se. In other words, don't completely deny your gerbils a food

Feed your gerbils at the same time every day as they like regular schedules. Always remove uneaten food, especially soft fruits like banana, grape and pear, and vegetables.

they love—just use a little discretion in doling out the seeds.

Vegetables: The second area of some caution in the gerbil's food plan is vegetables. As much as gerbils enjoy them—and need them, for their valuable vitamin and mineral contents and other benefits—too much can have negative effects. The high water content of vegetables can trigger digestive problems, diarrhea, and excessive urination if large amounts are ingested. Gerbils are desert dwellers, after all, so their need for moisture is minimal. Don't overdo it!

In terms of lettuce—another welcome and much-enjoyed food—give no more than a single, average-sized leaf, and not more often than every other day. Be sure to wash lettuce and other vegetables, as even small traces of pesticide can have severe consequences for the animals. It's

also important to *dry* washed vegetables thoroughly. Otherwise, the already high water intake will be increased, making potential problems much more likely.

Besides lettuce, gerbils also enjoy carrots (good for teeth, but remove the green parts), cucumbers, cabbage, cauliflower, broccoli, celery, turnips, beets, peas, tomatoes, red peppers, parsley, and parsnips.

Gerbils also enjoy certain wild plants—dandelions, clover, green grass, shepherd's purse *(Capsella bursa pastoris),* hogweed (ragweed, knotweed), yarrow *(Achillea milefolium),* coltsfoot *(Tussilago farfara),* chickweed *(Stellaria media),* bullweed *(Centaurea nigra),* and others. For obvious reasons, however, don't pick *any* plant for gerbil consumption unless you are absolutely sure of its identity.

By the same token, do not take plants from any area that may have been treated with pesticides or herbicides, for these are toxic, as are roadside plants that have been blanketed with car exhaust fumes. As with store-bought vegetables, wash and dry wild plants thoroughly.

Snacks: Another, more obvious area of dietary concern is snacks. It's all right to give gerbils an occasional potato chip or cookie (except those containing chocolate), but *only* occasionally, as these goodies offer little nutritional value. Less fattening but welcome alternatives are crackers, pretzels, bread crusts, and popcorn. Gerbils will also heartily accept cheese, bits of potato, meat (always cooked), and even dog biscuits.

Fresh fruit is probably the best snack of all. Gerbils readily accept pieces of apple, pear, banana, orange, avocado, strawberries, raspberries, and plums.

Adult gerbils will also eat mealworms, grasshoppers, and crickets, which are available in many pet stores; but most gerbil owners dislike the idea of dealing with insects, let alone live ones. For those who dare, it's best to buy the insects rather than collecting them in the wild, unless you are in an area remote enough that you can feel confident they have not been exposed to pesticides (good luck!).

Finally, gerbils will also greatly appreciate twigs (fruit trees, maple, beech, hazelnut willow) and hay for nibbling and gnawing.

Various nutritional supplements, which are mixed into everyday food, are available in pet stores, but these are rarely needed if a well-balanced diet is otherwise maintained.

Feeding Routine

Gerbils need be fed only once a day: morning, evening, or in between; the exact time doesn't really matter, though it's best (for you and them) to establish a routine and stick to it. Many pet owners prefer to take care of the responsibility in the morning (assuming that's when they start their day), because this is a time when many other daily routines are being satisfied—making coffee, getting ready for work, and so on—and it's just a matter of adding one more relatively quick, simple task. It also lets you get this duty "out of the way," so to speak, so you don't have to feel guilty if you come home late. You'll notice, by the way, that your pets will come to sense when it's feeding time, becoming increasingly anxious and active as they await your arrival.

It's fun to watch gerbils eat, deftly handling their food and buzzing away at it with their powerful jaws (wait till you see their precision in stripping sunflower seeds!). Note, however, that gerbils display a wide variety of eating patterns: some will immediately devour all or most of what you give them; others will prefer to nibble at their food

periodically throughout the day. Likewise, some gerbils will always eat one particular food item first (because they like it), or they may boycott certain items entirely (because they don't). This is all perfectly normal, as long as you continue to provide a well-balanced diet. Don't forsake nutrition merely to satisfy your pets' personal preferences. If the animal continually avoids certain foods, try replacing them with some of the many available alternatives (you should be doing that from time to time anyway). If that doesn't help, it may be time to consider a nutritional supplement.

Always provide only the freshest foods available; and, in the case of vegetables, fruits, and other foods that spoil quickly, always remove the previous day's leftovers before feeding anew. As a matter of routine maintenance, if the cage contains a nesting box, check it periodically to make sure that no food has been dragged in and abandoned there. Gerbils won't normally eat contaminated food, but it can sicken those that do. In time, you will be better able to estimate the amounts of food to give, so this should gradually become less of a concern.

Gerbils, as you have already learned, are basically clean animals, so it's all right to place lettuce, carrots, and other such larger-than-average offerings directly on the floor bedding (they'll probably end up there anyway). Seeds and other more manageable items belong in a dish or hopper, which should be cleaned thoroughly once a week.

So should the water bottle, and replace the contents while you're at it. At the same time, inspect the rubber stopper for leaks and the metal nozzle for sharp edges, which may have been caused by an overzealous nibbler. Stoppers can easily be replaced; sharp edges, filed down. If your water bottle has a glass nozzle, do not attempt to repair chips or cracks—get a new one.

Gerbils almost never fight over food, but there are times when you may witness a skirmish—if one of them is inadvertently or otherwise blocking access to food, for example, or (a more serious situation) if you have been feeding a consistently boring diet over a long period of time and suddenly toss in something new and excitingly different. The latter situation is asking for trouble; it also means you haven't been doing a good job taking care of your pets.

You should be experimenting with different foods—modestly, at any rate—as a matter of course. Don't think of this as a chore; it can be fun to introduce new foods and to observe how your pets react to them. If it helps, keep a record of what foods you've tried and how well they were accepted.

Vacation Time

Sooner or later, you'll be going away on vacation. No problem: you can easily leave gerbils unattended for up to a week, as long as you replace old bedding and provide fresh food and water before you leave. At the same time, assure yourself that the cage is indeed escapeproof, and that it is resting in a place where it won't be subject to direct sunlight or to drafts and extremes of temperature.

My Tip: If you want to go away for more than a week, you'll have to beg or bribe someone to change the bedding and replenish the food and water. Don't trust instructions to memory, especially if, as is likely, you are dealing with someone who is unfamiliar with gerbils. Write everything down, and be specific.

Signs of Nutritional Imbalance

Nutritional imbalance will manifest itself most visibly in the gerbil's fur. If the animal's coat loses its sheen, if its hair starts falling out and what appears to be a rash develops on its skin, then it's time to get nutritional supplements, or at least make drastic changes in diet. If you act early, the condition can reverse itself rather quickly. If you see no improvement, don't hesitate to seek the help of a veterinarian. In advanced cases of nutritional deficiency, gerbils lose mobility in their hind legs, in which case they must be taken to a veterinarian as soon as possible.

Diarrhea, often the result of wet or spoiled food, quickly robs a gerbil's body of valuable nutrients. Should this condition occur, stop moist foods for a few days, and evaluate the need for vitamin drops to help restore body reserves. Note also that floor dressing and/or nesting material must be changed at least once a day as long as the condition persists, and that food dishes should be cleaned with hot water, also every day. After the animal has recovered, clean the entire cage with disinfectant.

Obesity is another result of nutritional imbalance—too much fat and carbohydrates. If you see that the animals are becoming too heavy, put them on a diet, moderately restricting their intake of these essential ingredients until the situation corrects itself. You might also consider letting the animals out of their cage more often, or for longer intervals, so they have the opportunity for extra exercise. Every little bit helps.

More information on exercise can be found in the following chapter.

Handling

Taming Your Gerbil and Making Friends

The gerbil's innate sense of curiosity and its friendly attitude toward people generally make taming a painless process, provided that you apply a little common sense, buffered with gentleness, patience, and understanding.

Your mission, quite simply, is to gain your new pets' trust and confidence. The way to do this is through frequent contact with the animals. As they learn, through positive reinforcement, that the funny-looking giant snooping around their cage is not to be feared, they will gradually warm to your friendly advances, and the basis for your relationship will be formed.

After giving your new pets at least one day to recover from the trip home (and to get used to their new cage and new surroundings), you should take every opportunity to interact with them, except, of course, when they are sleeping—no one likes a rude awakening!

The importance of maintaining a patient attitude, especially during the initial phases of your mutual introduction, cannot be overstated. If, at this stage, you frighten, annoy, or somehow hurt the animal, it will be difficult to reverse the damage and set your relationship on its proper course.

Start by slowly putting your hand in the cage, in a nonthreatening way, allowing the animals to approach it and become familiar with its shape and scent. Don't be concerned if one of them climbs on top of your hand (consider it a sign of progress), and

don't panic if it starts to lick your skin—you won't catch anything. Repeat this exercise a few times during the first couple of days, but keep each encounter brief to minimize any stress you may cause the animals.

It's important that you make no sudden movements during these initial contacts. At the same time, it would be unfair not to warn you that some gerbils may display a tendency to nibble your fingers, though typically without inflicting injury. This can be due to a protein deficiency in the diet, or to an aggressive reaction triggered by recollection of

Introduce yourself to your new pets by slowly putting your hand in the cage—in a nonthreatening manner. Allow the animals to approach it and become familiar with its shape and scent. Don't be alarmed if the animals start climbing on your hand.

previous mistreatment at the hands of a former caretaker, or perhaps is nothing more than a manifestation of the animal's natural nibbling instinct. Whichever the case, your immediate reaction will obviously be to move your hand out of harm's way; try to do so calmly, without hurting or frightening the animal.

After your gerbils seem to have adjusted to your occasional presence, rest your hand on the bottom of the cage and see if you can get one of them to climb onto your open palm. This shouldn't be too difficult, as they are bound to feel the urge to examine you more closely sooner or later. (If you want to speed up the process, you can put a few sunflower seeds or other goodies on your hand.) When one of the gerbils is firmly settled in your palm, raise your hand slowly a few inches, without removing it from the cage, and then carefully lower the animal to the floor again. If your pet doesn't hop off right away, repeat the exercise; then try it with another animal. The point of all this, in addition to simple interaction, is to help dispel the animals' fear of being lifted up, at the same time reinforcing the notion that you do not represent a threat to their safety.

At feeding time, extend your benevolent provider image by continuing to offer food from your hand. At this point, you should have no difficulty in petting the animals. Do so deliberately and gently, rubbing or lightly scratching the head, ears, and back.

Playing/Exercising

Obviously, "play" with a gerbil is a different, more subtle type of interaction than you can have with a pet dog. A gerbil won't chase a ball or retrieve a stick (not even a twig) or run a few laps with you (though it will run about *on* your lap).

Nevertheless, play activity is important for at least one obvious and very practical reason: it gives the animal exercise. Because your gerbils will spend most of their time in the confinement of the cage or aquarium you provide them, their activity level will be greatly diminished compared to that of their counterparts in the wild. To stay fit, they need to burn off the extra calories they take in, which otherwise remain stored in their bodies in the form of fat.

Playing Inside the Cage

Left to their own devices, gerbils—like all mammals, including human beings—will regularly indulge their natural urge for physical activity, even in the confines of a cage. One favorite pastime is climbing up the sides of the cage (unfortunately, not possible with aquarium-type dwellings), and many times you'll find them hanging upside down from the roof—an amusing and somewhat surprising testimony to the gerbil's agility.

You may also witness occasional playfighting, not unlike the kind dogs display. Don't be alarmed by such antics; these mock-heroic "battles," which rarely resemble anything more than a cross between a slow dance and a wrestling match, aren't likely to escalate to serious levels. The animals are simply having fun, and at the same time testing each other's physical prowess.

You can do much to encourage physical activity inside your gerbils' cage; here are two simple ways to get them off to a flying start. First, provide as large an environment as you possibly can. Obviously, the more room the animals have, the more they will move about. Cramped quarters will only contribute to laziness—and the accumulation of fat!

Second, fill the cage with plenty of opportunities for diversion; in fact, make it a veritable obstacle course (within reason). Buy a few toys, as

To pick up a gerbil, cup your hand and scoop it up.

discussed earlier, but don't stop there. Place a cardboard tube or pipe on the floor of the cage; the animals love to crawl through "tunnels." You can put a large stone or brick inside as well, so the animals can climb up on it when the urge strikes them. A thick section of tree branch will work equally well, but it must be carefully positioned—bolted or tied down, if necessary—so that it cannot tip over, no matter how vigorously it may be used.

Actually, you can serve several needs at once if you put a small nesting box or similar type of shelter in one corner of the cage. Your pet will have a "cave" to hide out or relax in.

HOW-TO: Picking Up and Holding a Gerbil

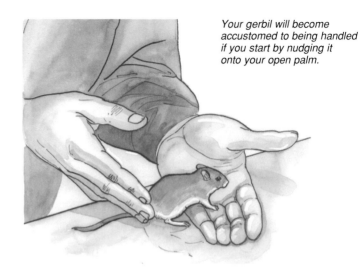

Your gerbil will become accustomed to being handled if you start by nudging it onto your open palm.

Using a Container

The easiest and safest way to pick up a gerbil—and the only way an inexperienced person (including your vacation-time caretaker) should do so—is to gently nudge it into a clean,

An easy way to get gerbils back into their cage is to tempt them into investigating a cardboard tube. When one of them crawls inside, you can seal off the ends with your hands, then transport the tube to the cage.

empty can with no sharp edges, or other suitable container (a small box or cardboard tube will do nicely) and to transport it to its cage in this fashion.

Using Your Hands

When you feel more comfortable with the animals—and they with you—you can pick them up directly with your hands. One good way, similar to the method described above, is to nudge your pet onto your open palm and then place your other hand

over it (easy does it), covering the animal so it can't fall or break free. Another relatively easy way to take hold of a gerbil is to flank its body with both hands, slowly cupping them together at the bottom so that the animal is scooped up into your palms. Both of these meth-

ods are reasonably foolproof.

With a little experience, you'll develop a "feel" (pardon the pun) for the animals, being able to pick them up rather deftly, with just the right amount of pressure. (Too loose a grip invites escape or an accident; gripping too tightly will frighten

When you feel more comfortable with the animals—and they with you—you can pick them up with your hands. After nudging your pet onto your open palm, quickly place your other hand over it so the animal can't fall or break free.

the animal and may even injure it.) When you reach the expert stage, you shouldn't have any problem simply lowering your hand over your pet, wrapping your forefinger and thumb around its midsection, and lifting it onto the palm of your other hand.

Lifting by the Tail

There is some disagreement about the merits of yet another way to pick up a gerbil—namely, lifting it up by the tail. The idea is to take hold of the appendage at its base, where it is thickest, lifting the animal off the ground and directly onto the palm. This method works fine if it's done right. If not—that is, if the tail is grabbed anywhere but at the very base, either because the handler misjudges or because the pet resists capture—there is a very real possibility of injuring the animal. Extremely fragile, the tail can tear, fracture, or, in the worst of scenarios, actually break off. Any of these misfortunes will of course cause the gerbil a great deal of pain and discomfort; it is also likely to affect the tail's function as a stabilizer, in addition to marring the animal's natural beauty.

Although many handlers insist there is absolutely no danger in picking up a gerbil by its tail if it is done correctly, the fact remains that accidents can (and do) happen, even if only to the inexperienced handler. At

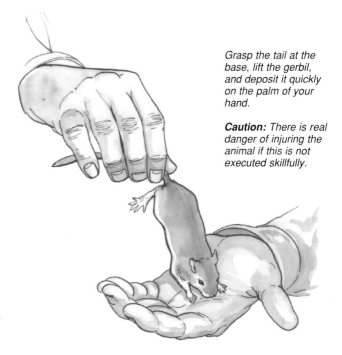

Grasp the tail at the base, lift the gerbil, and deposit it quickly on the palm of your hand.

Caution: *There is real danger of injuring the animal if this is not executed skillfully.*

the same time, considering that there are other, safer and simpler ways to handle your pet, it simply doesn't make sense to take chances, however confident you may feel about your manual dexterity.

Special Precautions When Lifting a Gerbil

In three areas of handling, there is unanimous agreement: first, never pick up a gerbil without providing a sturdy support underneath its body, be it your palm, a container of some kind, or whatever (in fact, if you are only transferring a gerbil from one cage to another—during cage cleaning, for instance—it's a good idea to make the switch from a position close to the floor or above a table, in case of an accident); second, never turn a gerbil onto its back, exposing its belly (this is true of many animals—the danger is that it may panic); and, finally, never pick up a gerbil by the scruff of its neck (you can hurt or panic the animal—or both).

The gerbil is inside a plastic ball (with air holes!). Pet shops have all kinds of toys for gerbils but by using your imagination you can make various toys for them yourself.

Cage Safety

Before proceeding further, a few reminders are in order.

• Check everything you intend to put in the cage for sharp edges, which can injure the animals.

• File down or otherwise neutralize potentially hazardous items.

• Note also that supplying raised platforms or other perches that the animals can climb on (and leap from) demands that cages be covered, as they should be anyway (preferably with wire mesh).

Finally, don't be dismayed when you notice that the wooden and cardboard items you so lovingly collected have

started to disintegrate from gnawing— gerbils won't be able to resist, meaning that some playthings will have to be replaced from time to time.

Playing Outside the Cage

Another great way to exercise your gerbils is by letting them out of the cage once in a while so they can run at large. A single room is sufficient— indeed, is preferable, since the animals will be easier to locate should you temporarily lose sight of them. Close doors or erect barricades to prevent access to other rooms.

Only adult gerbils should be allowed this form of recreation, and only those that are hand tame, that is, are not afraid to be touched or picked up. Otherwise, getting them back into the cage will be lots of exercise for *you!*

Choose a room that doesn't have a lot of hiding places. Gerbils are fond of exploring every nook and cranny they stumble upon; and if there are enough of them, you may have a tough time keeping track of your pets. For example, the kitchen is generally not a good place to let the animals roam, because they may end up behind your stove or refrigerator, where, for all practical purposes, they are inaccessible.

When sealing off a room, keep in mind that your purpose is not only to keep your gerbils inside, but also to keep any other pets you may have— cats, especially, but also dogs, other types of small animals, even birds— outside. To put it mildly, gerbils aren't fond of circuses, especially since their very lives may be in danger around these other animals. In fact, you should even go so far as to wash your hands before handling gerbils if you have recently handled other pets. Foreign scents can initiate a lot of tension.

Once the room is secure, place the cage on the floor in the center of the room and open its door. If the animals don't come out of their own volition,

This gerbil is shredding and rearranging paper—an excellent pastime. Don't give your pets cloth; they may try to eat it!

take them out yourself. Leave the cage on the floor, as this serves two purposes: it lessens the chance of a serious fall should one of the gerbils squirm free from your grasp during handling; it also provides the animals with a familiar haven to which to return—should they become frightened or for some reason suddenly decide they've explored enough for one day.

It's perfectly all right to let more than one gerbil out at a time, but try your best to keep an eye on them, for dangers lurk everywhere. For instance, gerbils don't leave their gnawing instincts in the cage when you let them out; and if they suddenly decide to sample an electric cord or a patch of paint that has become loose from the wall, someone must intervene. By the same token, your vigilance will also ensure that none of your furniture gets snacked upon. Wood is wood—gerbils don't make any distinctions as

far as presentation is concerned. They'll even gnaw on clothing if the opportunity presents itself.

For the most part, however, your pets will be content to simply stretch their limbs, occasionally running and leaping about as they indulge their curiosities and inspect the premises. You'll be amazed at how fast gerbils are, should you have the opportunity to see one going full throttle. No slouches, these animals have been known to outrun cats—of course, their lives usually depend on their doing so.

Some gerbils may become panic-stricken the first time they are exposed to the relatively wide expanse of an open room. In extreme cases, the animal can become so terrified as to be completely unable to move. If you experience such a situation, quickly return the gerbil to its cage, where it should soon recover. Wait a day or two before again trying to acclimate the animal to the world beyond its cage.

If you allow your pets to crawl up your sleeve or inside your shirt pocket, be aware that the animals' movements may become unbearably ticklish. Should you flinch or instinctively grab at them, you may hurt or panic them—or both.

Finding a "Lost" Gerbil

Don't panic if you suddenly discover that one of your gerbils is missing. If you start tearing the room apart, the animal is likely to react as if it were being hunted, as would not be far from the truth. Consequently, it will only burrow itself deeper into whatever secret lair it has uncovered.

Start by looking carefully around the area where you last remember seeing your pet. If it is nowhere to be found, all you can do is wait for it to reappear, as it will usually do when it is ready. Keep the room sealed, even if you have to leave for some reason; otherwise, you'll have no way of knowing that the animal hasn't found its way to a different part of the house, thereby complicating matters.

As long as the animal is missing, it's not a bad idea to leave some food out in the middle of the room. The gerbil will eventually get hungry, and the sight of food may help draw it out. Even if your pet manages to partake of the

Avoiding Accidents

Most accidents that befall gerbils occur when they are out of their cage. The pitfalls of picking up and holding gerbils, plus contact with other pets, sharp objects, electric cords, and toxins have already been discussed. A few more points need to be covered.

The first concerns heights. Should one of your pets end up on a bookshelf, table, or other "precipice," calmly retrieve it and place it back on the floor. Gerbils know their physical limits—they won't hurl themselves to their deaths trying to walk on air—but they *can* slip or stumble, and even a fall of several feet can be fatal.

Similarly, if, while playing with your pet, you allow it to crawl up your sleeve or inside your collar or shirt pocket, be aware that the animal's movements may become unbearably ticklish. This may sound like an amusing predicament, but if you flinch suddenly or instinctively grab at the animal, you may hurt or panic it, or do both.

Finally, although unlikely, it's not impossible that your pet gerbil's unquenchable curiosity may lead it to explore the contents of a vase, pail, or other water-filled container from which it may not be able to escape. Drownings have resulted from such unfortunate mishaps. Take the necessary precautions so that this tragedy won't happen in your household.

meal and vanish again without your noticing, at least you'll have the satisfaction of knowing that it is somewhere close by and that it's not starving.

If you have reason to believe that your pet has somehow found its way outdoors, be prepared for the worst.

You aren't likely to see it again, even if it isn't done in by cats or automobiles or inclement weather.

Tip: Don't get the impression that your gerbils will constantly be trying to escape from you. Tame animals will not. Typically, a missing animal has simply been carried away during one of its exploratory excursions and is soon located.

Biting and Aggressiveness

As mentioned earlier in this chapter, many gerbils will occasionally nip at their owners. Rarely, however, will they do so with enough force to break the skin; and even if they do draw a little blood, it's reassuring to know that these clean, farm-bred animals are not among the common carriers of the dreaded rabies virus. (Tetanus is a more valid concern if you haven't been vaccinated.)

The kind of biting behavior associated with the gerbil's natural tendency to nibble at things (which is genetic and, for the most part, unalterable), as well as the kind that may be attributed to insufficient amounts of protein in the diet (which is easily remedied by a change of diet), is basically aggression-free—pretty tame stuff, as "biting" goes.

More hazardous (and usually more painful) is the reactionary, genuinely aggressive biting reflex that manifests itself when a gerbil is frightened or feels threatened. For this reason you should never attempt to break up a fight between gerbils—even long-time pets—with your bare hands. (Use gloves or, if they aren't handy, anything nonlethal that will serve to divert their attention or to separate them; sometimes, just a little commotion on your part—a rap on the cage, some hearty vocalization—will do the trick.) You're also likely to get more than you bargained for if you try to take hold of a sleeping gerbil. This is not a wise move, for obvious reasons.

In terms of new arrivals in your home, keep in mind that it's only natural for the animals to be apprehensive until they get to know you. This can take a little time. Until they learn to accept you, don't be surprised if any display of overeagerness to "make friends" provokes a defensive reaction. For all they know, they may be your intended dinner!

As far as aggressive reactions caused by intentional abuse or even careless handling are concerned, such retaliation is justified. Gerbils are not toys; they won't tolerate mistreatment—not for long, anyway. At some point, they will be compelled to strike back.

Ailments and Injuries

Maintaining Good Health

The key to maintaining the health of your gerbils centers around concepts of prevention. Generally speaking, if you do your best to supply a balanced diet, make frequent water changes, keep the cage clean and protected from dampness, drafts, and extremes of temperature—70 to 75°F (21–23°C) is considered the ideal range—and provide opportunities for the animals to be happily occupied, you should have every reason to feel confident that your pets will reach their fullest potential.

Of course, ailments and injuries can still occur. For this reason it's important to monitor your animals' well-being with regular observations of behavior and, should your suspicions be aroused, careful physical inspection, followed by the initiation of whatever treatment is in the animals' best interest.

As far as diseases are concerned, pet gerbils rarely become ill. Part of the reason is that they are born and bred in controlled environments and, in the case of imported stock, are subjected to quarantine as well. This, coupled with their general cleanliness, improves the chances of good health considerably.

In-cage injuries often result from fighting. Typically, the opponents will be adults of the same sex, although females are also prone to thrash out at new mates. Outside the cage, accidents, discussed in preceding chapters, are the most likely source of injuries. As you already know, there is much you can and should do to avoid them.

Familiarity with your pets—the kind that comes from frequent interaction—is the best defense in maintaining your gerbils' health. Many signs of health problems and evidences of injuries are easily detected with the naked eye; still others may be revealed through a routine process of deduction based on evidence found in the animals' environment.

For example, a healthy gerbil is active and alert, its eyes are clear and bright, its fur is smooth and glossy. If you notice, as indeed you should, that the animal has become lethargic and withdrawn, that its eyes are runny and heavy-lidded, or that its fur is dull and uneven, these signs should tip you off that something is amiss.

Colds

Colds are among the most common ailments that gerbils suffer from, however infrequently, and they catch them the same way that people do—from contact with already afflicted individuals, or by overexposure to dampness, drafts, and low temperatures. The symptoms are familiar ones: runny eyes, a wet nose, chills, frequent sneezing. Lack of appetite is often apparent as well, and the animal may appear tired and weak.

The first step is to isolate sick animals so that the virus cannot contaminate others. A second cage, even a small one, will come in handy here; otherwise, you may be able to fashion a makeshift one from an old dresser drawer or even a couple of cardboard boxes (placed one inside the other,

Gerbils are hardy and active animals. To keep them healthy, provide a well-balanced diet and clean water every day, and clean the cage at least once a week. Anyone with a cold should keep away from gerbils!

A healthy gerbil is active and alert. If you notice that an animal has become lethargic and withdrawn, that its eyes are runny and heavy-lidded, or that its fur is dull and uneven, this should tell you that something is wrong.

they form a more substantial barrier against escape, at least for a while).

Provide the sick animal with all the comforts of home—food, water, bedding—and then leave it alone, allowing nature to take its course. If your pet stays warm, dry, and comfortable, the condition should pass in a matter of days.

If it does not, or appears to worsen, you can treat the animal with an antibiotic, which is added to drinking water. A word of caution: Don't go to your medicine cabinet for help; go to a veterinarian. Always be careful to administer drugs only as directed.

Another treatment for colds involves wiping the animal's nose with eucalyptus oil or other aromatics. Although this won't cure your pet of its ailment, it will make the animal feel better by temporarily slowing the glands responsible for mucus production, bringing some relief to the body's overburdened respiratory system.

As a preventive measure, you can't do better than to add cod-liver oil or vitamin drops to your pets' food. These help in that they support the animals' own internal disease fighting mechanisms.

If, in spite of your best efforts, one or more of your pets fall prey to a cold, it would be wise to consider whether the cage is indeed in the best possible location. For instance, maybe it's too close to a window (or too far from a heat source), or perhaps your own heating or air-conditioning habits are to blame. Consider the possibilities, and if you have any doubts, experiment by moving the cage to another, well-thought-out location.

Diarrhea and Constipation

If one of your pets comes down with *diarrhea,* you'll know it, even before you sight the evidence. The message to your nose will be loud and clear. Although this malady is more likely to affect newborns and young animals, it occurs in all age groups from time to time.

Diarrhea is usually the result of improper feeding. Specifically, the causes are most often reduced to spoiled food, an overabundance of greens or other high-water-content vegetables, or greens that have not been allowed to dry. In the first instance, regular inspection of food supplies is dictated. Use your nose to help detect bad food; also, look for defects in packaging, packaging dates, and contamination by moisture, mold, or vermin. If the source of the problem still eludes you, make a careful inspection of the cage. It's possible that a portion of food served earlier somehow became buried under bedding, only to be discovered—and consumed—after it had become stale.

While typically not life-threatening, or even highly contagious (though indeed it can be passed from one animal to another), diarrhea is certainly a major discomfort to the animal. It also robs the body of fluids and essential minerals and vitamins, making the gerbil more susceptible to other, more serious ailments. For these reasons, it is important to take prompt action when the condition occurs.

The best approach is to isolate the animal and place it on a diet of dry foods exclusively until the situation corrects itself, usually within 48 hours. If no change is apparent after two days, take the animal to a veterinarian; there may be other, more complicated problems with your pet's health. At the very least, your vet will be able to prescribe medication or other form of treatment to speed up recovery.

One last, unwelcome task remains. To prevent the recurrence of this unpleasant problem, it is recommended that you clean the cage thoroughly, including food bowls and whatever utensils are used to deliver food. If the outbreak was widespread or otherwise severe, clean the entire cage from top to bottom, using hot water and a disinfectant.

At this time, it would also be wise to review your pets' diet (and your own habits regarding food presentation) to make sure that you yourself have not contributed to the problem. If you have, but don't make the necessary adjustments to correct matters, you're bound to experience more outbreaks in the future.

Constipation is a far less frequent occurrence, but it is also more difficult to diagnose, since a paucity or absence of waste droppings offers the first clue that this condition has manifested itself. Furthermore, if you have more than a pair of animals, it may be entirely impossible to detect that a single one of them is having difficulty of this type.

That is unfortunate because, however rare this condition may be, it sometimes signals the start of what may turn out to be a life-threatening situation. Occasionally, constipation is the result of eating an inappropriate food, such as chocolate or other sweets. In such instances, there is

no great cause for alarm, as the gerbil will probably survive the experience with little more than temporary discomfort.

A much more dangerous scenario occurs when the source of the problem turns out to be the animal's ingestion of wool, including wool blends, or similar materials whose fibers are likely to collect in the intestine. The materials in question may have inadvertently been placed in the cage in the form of bedding material, or the animal may have chewed on something made of wool while it was allowed to roam (unsupervised, apparently) outside of its cage.

Should total blockage of the intestine occur, the stomach will start to enlarge, eventually swelling to the point where it may actually rupture, killing the animal. Because gerbils are avid chewers, the aforementioned fabrics should *never* be used in the cage (see page 23 for appropriate bedding materials).

Milder forms of constipation can be treated with a change of diet. Because the object in this case is *to increase* the moisture content in the intestine, the first step is to provide more greens and other vegetables at the expense of dry food. You can also supply a small amount of milk, as it is known to promote a loosening of the bowels. If these methods don't work, there's one more thing you can try before you call in the vet—castor oil. Use no more than a single drop, however.

Mange

Mange is a disease caused by parasitic mites that embed themselves into an animal's skin, then lay eggs and die. As the new generation matures, it spreads itchy lesions across the body, at the same time causing loss of fur. The greatest danger related to this affliction is the secondary bacterial infections that can take root in inflamed skin. These can sometimes be fatal.

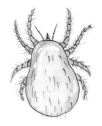

Mange is caused by parasitic mites that embed themselves into the gerbil's skin, then lay eggs and die. As the new generation matures, it spreads itchy lesions across the body, at the same time causing loss of fur.

There are two basic types of mange, wet and dry. The former variety forms as blisters that eventually break, release their fluids, and turn into sores. Typically occurring around the ears, feet, and rump, the condition depletes hair to the extent that bald patches soon form across these areas.

Dry mange is not much kinder, although it's somewhat deceptive in that initial hair loss is more gradual. Unfortunately, the damage is usually well under way by the time most keepers realize what is happening, which is that, in addition to the loss of fur, tiny particles of skin are continuously flaking off the animal's body. Your pet facilitates the process by constantly scratching away at troubled areas.

The most likely source of mange will be any new arrivals you may subsequently acquire. Always examine them carefully before any kind of contact is initiated with the rest of your tribe, as mange is highly contagious. Afflicted animals should be isolated from the others immediately.

Note also that you must always wash your hands after handling an animal that is suspected of having mange since you can easily transmit the disease to other animals. To be extra safe, always take care of (presumably) healthy stock before tending to ill animals.

Treatment for mange involves the application of commercial preparations specially formulated to destroy mites without harming the pet. These are available at most pet stores. As always, read instructions carefully and follow them to the letter. To be on the safe side, you'll also have to sanitize the cage and treat it with an appropriate pesticide.

Be aware that not all skin and coat problems are caused by mange. Some may simply be due to vitamin deficiencies (vitamin C in particular), especially in younger animals. It's also possible that the source of complaint may be a bacterial infection entirely independent of mange. Such an invasion often starts around the nose, eventually progressing to the stomach and legs. Both conditions are treatable (the former quite easily, with vitamin drops or a change of diet; the latter, with antibiotics or special dips), but in the case of bacterial infections early detection may be critical—another plus for the pet owner who makes

If you have a sick animal, isolate it from your other pets.

Healthy gerbils are alert and active, have bright, clear and wide-open eyes, while their ears stand up straight and their fur is clean and sleek.

regular, thorough observations of his or her stock.

Other Parasites

Fleas and lice: Mites are by no means the only parasites that can thrive at the expense of your pets. There are others, both external and internal in nature.

Joining mites in the *external* category are two additional well-known enemies: fleas and lice. Since they have outlasted even the mighty dinosaurs, there is virtually no reason to assume we will ever be rid of them. If there is any consolation, it is that their appearance among gerbils in controlled environments is rare. Once they have moved in, however, they aren't easy to evict.

If no peculiar physical manifestations are evident on an animal's body, constant scratching and biting at the skin will probably be the first signal that new tenants have arrived. Treatment involves the use of commercial dusting powders and sprays, available at any pet store. Do not, however, be tempted to use on your gerbils flea powders or other medications intended specifically for dogs. The mixture in these is too strong for small animals and can make them extremely ill.

Start on your pets first, working the pesticide well into the skin (per instructions, which usually require a second treatment later on, in case there were any survivors), then thoroughly clean and treat the cage. This means removing and destroying all bedding material

Even if no physical marks are apparent on the animal's body, constant scratching and biting at the skin will probably be the first sign that parasites have attacked your pet. Treatment involves the use of commercial dusting powders and sprays.

and floor dressing before dusting or spraying. Assuming the instructions on the label don't forbid it, mix a small amount of pesticide in with the new floor dressing. Also, be alert for new outbreaks—if you didn't do a thorough job, the pests will be back.

Internal parasites—worms, primarily—enter an animal's body through contaminated food. They start out as eggs but, nourished by the host animal's own nutrients and precious fluids, eventually hatch into their more familiar forms. At some point, your pet will expel the worm with its excrement, but by then the adult parasite will have planted new eggs, and the terrible cycle will be under way.

If you discover a worm in your pets' cage, isolate the infected animal, assuming you can determine which one it is (if you only have a pair, take your pick), then seek the help of a veterinarian. Worms are often fatal if left unchecked.

Unfortunately, where worms are concerned, seeking professional med-ical treatment is not enough. As with external parasites, you'll once more be faced with the task of cleaning the cage—only in this instance, uncompromised thoroughness is an absolute must. Certainly you'll have to destroy all bedding material and floor dressing, but instead of simply dusting or spraying with pesticides, you'll have to take more drastic measures. Here you have a choice: either you can obtain a blowtorch and sterilize the cage by running its flame over the entire surface; or else you can purchase a strong disinfectant such as phenol (also known as carbolic acid), and, mixing the compound with hot water in a vat or tub big enough to accommodate the whole cage, submerge it completely for at least 15 minutes. One can also use a hot soapy chlorine bleach solution to sanitize the cage. Actually, there is one other alternative, but it's more expensive—you can buy a new cage. As involved or unpleasant as the alternatives may seem, they are essential if you hope to prevent a recurrence of this plague upon your pets.

Vermin

Rats, mice, and other vermin are not parasites by definition. Like parasites, however, they are destructive and they perpetuate disease; also, they can be just as difficult to get rid of once they've laid claim to a new territory.

There are at least 500 varieties of rats in the world, and most of them have little effect on our lives. Two notable exceptions are the black rat *(Rattus rattus)* and the brown rat *(Rattus norvegicus),* both of the family Muridae. These two culprits are prolific and aggressive and eat practically anything, gerbil food included. Worst of all, the diseases they often carry can contaminate any food or animal, (or human being, for that matter) that they come into contact with.

Mice, most of which are members of the families Muridae and Cricetidae, are even more common. They, too, are omnivorous, are rapid breeders, and, like rats, can carry many types of diseases, including some that are harmful to people.

If any of these creatures can get inside your home, the first target will probably be food storage areas—that's why it's so important to keep these places as inaccessible as possible. If conditions allow, they'll also find their way to your gerbils' cage. Even if they can't get inside, at the very least they will frighten your pets severely, causing the animals great stress. In fact, female gerbils have been known to devour their young in what is believed to be a misguided defensive reaction to the presence of intruders.

Of course, for your sake as well as your gerbils', you'll want to take immediate action if you discover your home is beset with these unwelcome guests. Poisons and traps are the generally prescribed methods. Whether you take on the task yourself or call in a pest control company to do the job, be sure you understand what dangers, if any, the chemicals or traps being used may pose to your gerbils and any other household pets, so that you can take necessary precautions to protect their well-being. During this period, you'll also have to be especially vigilant when you let your gerbils out of the cage for their daily romps, not only because poisons or traps may be near, but also because their intended targets are no doubt lurking somewhere nearby.

Injuries

For better or for worse, there are relatively few courses of action available when dealing with an injured gerbil. If you notice, for example, that one of your pets is sporting what appears to be a minor wound, be it from fighting or accidental cause, all you can do is apply an antiseptic to the affected area and let the body heal itself as best it can. Most of the time, minor injuries heal rather quickly.

My Tip: Forget about applying dressings or bandages—human beings know that a wound heals more quickly, with less chance of infection, when it is covered; but to a gerbil, any such covering is nothing more than a challenge to be attacked by its ever-active teeth. Your labor of love will be chewed off and discarded in no time. Moreover, if you attempt to anticipate this reaction by wrapping the injury more securely or using extra amounts of tape, you risk making matters worse because your pet will only work that much harder to remove the covering, perhaps aggravating the wound in the process.

More serious injuries—especially those around the genitals, stomach, neck, and eyes—demand the professional scrutiny of a veterinarian. Don't try to play doctor yourself. Here again, you risk making matters worse by denying the animal the professional attention that it may need but you are not qualified to provide.

Similar rules apply to broken bones, more often than not the result of a fall. Minor fractures will heal themselves. Apart from continuing to provide essential nutrients in the form of a balanced diet, there is really nothing you can do to expedite recovery.

Unfortunately, more serious breaks are virtually impossible to set, as the animal neither will tolerate a splint or cast of any kind, nor will it sit still long enough to benefit from the healing process. If, in your vet's best judgment, this is indeed the case and the gerbil is locked in a hopeless cycle of pain and suffering, the only humane alternative is to have the animal put to sleep.

Eye Infections

There is one health problem that you *can* actively do something about—in fact, if you do not take action, serious complications are sure to follow. The problem is eye infections, typically occurring after a particle of sand, dirt, or some other foreign matter gets trapped behind what is known as the nictating (or nictitating) membrane, a transparent third eyelid located at the inner corner of the eye.

Not exclusive to gerbils, this membrane is found also on various birds and reptiles. Intended to protect the eye (gerbils do a lot of digging and burrowing), it actually has an opposite effect when it is invaded by any kind of debris. Trapped inside the membrane, these particles may cause irritation so severe that the animal can inflict serious damage to itself in trying to obtain relief. In fact, some animals have actually scratched out an eyeball in their frenzied attempts to relieve their suffering. Death soon follows.

Constant scratching in the eye region will be the first signal that something is wrong. If you don't take heed of the situation, you'll eventually notice that the animal has worn away some of the fur around its eyes. By this time, if not sooner, immediate action is called for. You can treat your pet by first bathing the eye with warm water (an eyedropper works best, but you can improvise if you don't have one handy), then applying an antibiotic eye lotion, which will help soothe the discomfort. Of course, if you don't feel confident to undertake this procedure yourself, by all means seek professional help.

Note also that some older gerbils develop a condition in which the eyes appear to be inflamed and the nictating membrane protrudes from its normal position. In most cases, this is not the result of debris in the eye, but rather is part of the normal and inevitable disintegration of the body as it succumbs to the aging process. No treatment is required.

Breeding

Initial Considerations

You might think that breeding gerbils is rather easy—they do most of the important work, after all—but it's not a project you should undertake lightly. As a responsible pet owner, you'll want to carefully consider the consequences of the biological forces you'll be setting into motion.

Certainly the opportunity to observe the phenomenon of reproduction and birth, even in animals at the lower end of the evolutionary spectrum, is a wondrous and fascinating thing, as well as a genuine learning experience for children, but have you given any thought as to what you will do with the four, six, eight, or more pups that each pair of adult gerbils is likely to produce?

A wise move, before breeding your pets, is to make inquiries—among friends, and even at local pet shops and schools—to see whether you'll find a ready home for the intended offspring. This will prevent a lot of headaches later on, as well as the guilt and sorrow associated with the realization that you may eventually have to have unwanted animals destroyed. After all, it's unlikely you'll want to or be able to keep them all.

Once you've cleared this initial hurdle, the next step is to make sure that you have a male and a female to pair together and that they will accept each other as mates.

Sexing and Pairing Gerbils

Determining Sex

Once gerbils have reached puberty, which occurs anywhere from the ninth through the twelfth week of life, sexing them is a rather routine matter. Since gerbils do not take kindly to being turned onto their backs, determining sex is one instance when it is advisable to pick the animal up at the base of the tail, raising it slightly off the ground until the area in question is in plain view. The scrotum of the male, clearly visible on the animal's underside, is represented by a dark, oblong-shaped sac just beneath the tail. Females, of course, do not bear this feature, and the vagina, close to the anus, is hardly noticeable by comparison. Once you see and note the dissimilarity, it is highly unlikely that you will ever mistake one sex for the other.

There are other differences between male and female gerbils, but none so

Gerbils generally choose one mate for life. Even if one of the partners dies, the remaining animal will probably not accept a new mate.

53

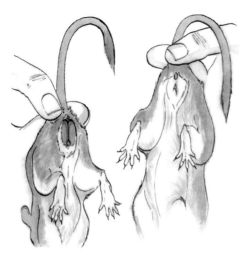

Once gerbils have reached puberty, sexing them is not difficult. The scrotum of the male (left), clearly visible on the animal's underside, is represented by a dark, oblong-shaped sac just underneath the tail. A female's underside (right) is much different—the vagina, close to the anus, is much less noticeable.

definitive or as readily discernible. Adult males are generally larger, for one thing, and the fur in back of their hind legs tends to have a tufted appearance. In addition, the area around the base of the male's tail is somewhat tapered, whereas the female's hindquarters are smoother and more rounded. Finally, in terms of behavior, males tend to be more domineering, but this distinction and others may be easily blurred under various circumstances, so they are not as conclusive as direct examination of the sexual organs.

Pairing Gerbils

The pairing of males and females is much easier if it is done before they are sexually mature—in other words, before three months of age. If you intended to breed the animals from the very beginning and therefore requested a mixed pair when you purchased them, pairing was done at the pet shop.

On the other hand, if you know from the start that you have no desire to breed the animals, you should buy a pair of the same sex—it's the only simple way to prevent breeding activity, short of separating the gerbils before they reach maturity, which is neither kind nor practical. Doing so deprives the animals of companionship; of course, it also means you'll have to purchase (and maintain) at least two separate cages.

It is always best to obtain gerbils from the same litter, especially if you do intend to breed them. Unrelated gerbils are often unwilling to accept each other, in which case fighting frequently results. Upon introduction, they will nervously sniff one another, usually without a show of aggression until one of them makes an advance or what is otherwise interpreted as a move to establish dominance—attempting to push the cage mate onto its back, for instance. At this point the fur begins to fly.

If you or an appointed caretaker is not present to quell the disturbance, the animals may very well fight to the death. At the very least, they can inflict serious damage on one another. Should you be present when fighting occurs, carefully separate the two, giving them at least a few days to forget the experience before attempting to reintroduce them. Next time, however, use the method described on page 11 of this book—that is, take your time, allowing brief, well-supervised encounters, including occasional swapping of cages, until the animals become accustomed to each other.

Note that fighting does not always occur when two gerbils are introduced. With a little luck, the animals, whether a mixed pair or members of the same sex, may accept each other from the outset. This is especially true if they have not yet reached puberty. In any event, once the animals have been successfully paired, there is little chance they will go to war with one another, although play-fighting and even an occasional minor skirmish are probably inevitable.

The Basics of Breeding

There are a number of things you can do to encourage successful breeding. If you have heeded the advice in earlier chapters, you are already aware of the importance of providing your pets with sufficient cage space, plus proper bedding and/or nesting material. For breeding purposes, it is even more important that these basic comforts be available.

To a great extent, successful breeding is also contingent upon the animals having a certain amount of privacy. For this reason, it's best to move the cage to an area of the home where noise and human interference are likely to be at a minimum. By the same token, since females generally come into heat (estrus) in the late afternoon or early evening hours, it's best to avoid disturbing them late in the day.

Gerbils in captivity are capable of breeding at any time of the year, provided that conditions are right. In other words, their breeding cycle is not a seasonal one, as it is with many other animals. Nevertheless, it has been observed that breeding occurs with greater frequency during summer months, with a corresponding decline in activity in the winter. Statistically, litters born in the summer months also tend to be larger in number than those born at other times of the year, though exceptions can and do occur.

It is estimated that females come into heat approximately every five to ten days from the time they are sexually mature until anywhere between 14 and 20 months of age. During this time, as many as ten litters may be produced by a single female, with each litter consisting of one to ten pups (the average is four or five). As females age, the frequency of birth, as well as the size of the litters, decreases gradually until reproductive activity ceases.

A male gerbil's fertility usually outlasts that of a female. Even though some male gerbils in the wild are believed to mate with several different females, pairs in captivity almost always stay together for their entire lives.

Pet owners who wish to breed several pairs of gerbils at the same time may be relieved to learn that it is not necessary to provide separate cages for each parental unit. Instead, a colony arrangement is the sensible way to go. You can start with two or three pairs, or even a single pair. In the latter case, all you need do is leave the initial offspring in the same cage with the parents until the pups mature and start producing litters of their own. It won't be long before you have a full-fledged colony on your hands, assuming that the cage you have provided is of sufficient size. When conditions start to get crowded, the gerbils themselves will take matters under control, automatically ceasing to breed to ensure their own survival.

The colony approach to breeding does have a few potential pitfalls, and it is important that you be aware of them. For instance, if cage space is sufficient and breeding activity is allowed to continue unchecked, it's not unlikely that females will embark on a second pregnancy right after their first litters are born. The concern here, considering that the gestation period is a comparatively scant 24 to 28 days, is that the second broods will arrive before members of the first litters are fully independent. As a result, half-grown youngsters, still dependent on their mothers to a certain extent, will be kicked out of their nests to make room for new arrivals. The females' instinctive concern for their new broods will outweigh the needs of their initial offspring. In rare cases, these older youngsters may be perceived as nuisances to the extent that some of them may be killed by angry parents. At the very least, they are likely to become victims of neglect.

If limited breeding is desired, separate males and females a few days before the first litter is due. This will prevent the second mating from taking place. Should you decide you want another litter later on, you can reunite the parents; but be advised that there is a good chance that the two will fight, especially if the male is placed in what has become the female's cage. Often, the female will attack the male without any provocation. You might have better success by placing the female inside the male's cage. Even so, be prepared for the worst. If hostility resumes, your only alternative is to separate the animals and, after a reasonable "cooling off" period, begin the introduction process from scratch, as if they were meeting for the very first time.

Tip: An easy way to avoid these confrontations is to breed new stock from the litter that has just arrived. Of course, this means that you'll have to wait a few months until the young have matured.

Courtship and Mating

After you have successfully paired two intended parents, don't be concerned if mating does not occur right away. Although gerbils are physically ready to produce litters by the time they are three months old, only in one out of three pairings will breeding actually commence at this age. In the majority of cases, the animals will approach six months of age before the first litter arrives, so be a little patient and by all means continue to maintain optimum conditions in terms of comfort and privacy. As far as diet is concerned, continue to provide the same well-balanced selection of foods that you always do, with the single exception of increasing protein-rich items at the expense of foods high in fat content.

Mating usually takes place in the early evening hours, but can occur at practically any time. Couplings are brief in duration, but they are usually repeated several times during any given session. Pet owners who wish to observe the mating ritual need only watch and wait, although it's important to maintain a reasonable distance from the cage so as not to disturb the animals.

One unmistakable clue that something may be about to happen is the rhythmic thumping of the hind legs by the male, this being a physical manifestation of the animal's excitement. If the female is ready and willing to accept him, she will respond by presenting her hindquarters to him. The male then mounts the female, and mating begins.

Pregnancy

If you know from observation that the sex act has occurred, or if you believe (or even suspect) that mating has taken place unnoticed, it is a good idea to begin adding dry powdered milk to the animals' food, primarily for the sake of the mother-to-be, since her reserve of nutrients will be taxed as the gestation process gets under way.

If you haven't already done so, now is also the time to cut down on sunflower seeds, the most fattening of gerbil foods. By the time the litter arrives—some three or four weeks from the outset—females often double in weight anyway. It is important to add, however, that in some cases—for instance, when the female is large to begin with—it's possible that you won't notice much weight gain. That's not to say it isn't occurring; you just can't see it. The only foolproof way to confirm pregnancy in such cases is to weigh the animal before mating occurs and then a week or two after gestation is believed to have begun. Do not, however, abuse this practice. Weigh the animal early in the suspected pregnancy, and only once or twice. It's best to avoid handling females when gestation is well under way.

Nesting Material

You may choose to provide the female with a nesting box in one corner of the cage (if you do, make sure that the doorway is big enough to accommodate her when she is bulging with babies), but it may be to your advantage *not* to do so. A nesting box isn't mandatory, and it will obscure your view of the events taking place inside it.

A better alternative is to provide strips of burlap, paper, or other suitable materials (see page 26), so the animals can fashion their own nest. They will do so eagerly, affording you the opportunity to appreciate their construction skills. Except when they are nursing, mothers usually keep their babies covered with nesting material, but you may be able to catch a glimpse of them at other times as well. Observing the animals is valuable not only from an educational standpoint, but also for monitoring the health and well-being of both mother and offspring. This is especially important when the litter in question is the mother's first, as inexperienced females are sometimes not fully attentive to maternal duties. The same may be true of older females that are past their reproductive prime.

Caution: If the mother starts moving her pups to a new location in the cage, it may be a signal that your too frequent presence is disturbing her.

The Birthing Period

Although the young may arrive at any time of day, more often than not

Gerbils will gladly fashion their own nest. Give them sufficient material to work with, but don't concern yourself with shredding it. The animals are well-equipped to do this task by themselves.

they will do so during the night or early morning hours. Birth occurs without fanfare, so if you are sleeping, you won't learn of the event until the next morning, when you'll hear faint, high-pitched squeaks emanating from the cage.

You may feel a little disappointed that you weren't able to witness the birth, but it's probably just as well that the mother didn't have to concern herself with this intrusion. Even the male gerbil keeps his distance at this stage. As for assisting with the birthing process, this is not necessary. Complications almost never occur, and even if the litter is a large one, the entire procedure rarely lasts more than an hour.

The survival rate for newborns is in the vicinity of 75 percent, so don't be alarmed if you find one or two lifeless pups in the cage. And don't feel guilty either. Such deaths are almost always the result of congenital problems that are beyond anyone's control. The same applies in cases where the litter is a small one, numbering only one or two pups. For reasons not fully understood, these offspring rarely live very

57

Newborn gerbils are completely defenseless.

long. All you can do is remove the dead pups and dispose of them.

Newborn gerbils come into the world hairless, blind, deaf, and toothless. As such, they are completely defenseless, relying for survival entirely upon their mother's milk and good intentions. Approximately 1 inch (2.5 cm) long at birth, a typical pup weighs a mere 0.1 ounce (approximately 2.8 g). It's too early, at this point, to concern yourself about the sex of the pups, but just for the record, statistics show that the ratio in any given litter almost always works out to about half male, half female.

As you might imagine, the first week of life is critical for newborn gerbils. Perhaps ironically, it's also a time when human contact should be avoided as much as possible. As protective as the mother may be, she is also nervous and easily frightened during this period—so much so that she may smother, trample, or even desert her litter, unintentionally or otherwise, if she feels harassed.

Cannibalism

High levels of stress can even trigger cannibalistic behavior. This is not terribly common, but it does occur. More often than not, it is the presence of other animals—cats, mice, rats, and so on—that incites this reaction, but even human interference can be the cause. Unfortunately, there is no distinct pattern to the problem. Some mothers will destroy a single pup each day; others will wipe out the entire litter in one rampage.

To complicate matters, cannibalism can even occur when there is no perceived threat from outside sources.

They rely on their mother for food and protection.

Some experts contend that it sometimes represents a kind of "mercy killing," the result of a female's inability to raise her young (when she is unable to produce milk, for example). Excessive inbreeding may also have something to do with it. Worst of all, the trait is often passed on to surviving female offspring, so forget about breeding any female exposed to this behavior. It is a difficult habit to control.

Sometimes males too are guilty of cannibalism. It may very well be that a first-time father resents what he sees as an intrusion into his established territory. In defense of the male, however, it should be said that he usually makes a decent parent, helping to build the nest and otherwise looking after the newborns when and if the need arises.

Low-protein diets have also been blamed for cannibalism, and it has

even been suggested that the eating of pups that have died of natural causes may simply be an instinctive reaction. Most of the time, pups that die prematurely are simply left alone, as if the parents know that you, the owner, will deal with the situation eventually; sometimes, however, the parents will actually attempt to "bury" dead pups themselves.

As a countermeasure to cannibalism, all you can do is count the number of offspring as soon as possible after birth, without touching them, so that you can keep track of them as they develop. If a pup disappears and you fear the worst, remove the male from the cage. If the female continues to raise and care for her young without further incident, it is likely that the male was the culprit. If, however, the female proves to be the guilty party,

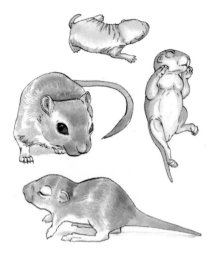

Born hairless, deaf, blind, and without teeth, gerbils nevertheless grow quickly. By the time pups are three days old, their once pink skin will have begun turning dark; around the fifth or sixth day, they will be covered with a light mantle of fur; sometime between the tenth and twelfth day, their eyes will open and the youngsters will begin to resemble their parents.

Newborns are completely defenseless, relying entirely upon their mother's milk and good intentions for survival. As soon as the litter arrives, increase the mother's food ration, as she will need all the strength and nourishment she can get to provide and care for her pups.

then you have a serious problem on your hands, for she must now be separated from her pups, however bleak will be their chances for survival.

Despite the somber sentiments of the last few paragraphs, do not go overboard and become paranoid about the possibility of cannibalism. Agonizing over it will drive you crazy! Certainly it's important that you be aware of it, because it can indeed happen, but recognize that it is the exception, not the rule, among gerbils. If the trait manifests itself in spite of your best efforts to keep the animals comfortable and stress-free, it can only be considered an act of fate. Deal with it as best you can, and focus your attention on the needs of the living.

My Tip: As soon as the litter arrives, increase the female's food ration, as she will need all the strength (and nourishment) she can muster to provide and care for her pups. The animals, you will notice, grow quickly.

Raising the Young

The First 21 Days

By the time the pups are three days old, their once pink skin will have begun to turn dark, and they will be making clumsy crawling movements, with limited success. Around the fifth or sixth day, they will be covered with a light mantle of fur. Though the pups are still blind, their ears will be fully functional.

Sometime between the tenth and the twelfth day, the newborns' eyes will open, although a few more days will be required until they actually begin to see well. By this time, their fur will have assumed its true color, and the pups will begin to resemble their parents, except that the tail and limbs may be slightly underdeveloped. Never fear: these will fill out by the time the animals mature.

Gerbils seem to display their innate inquisitiveness early in life, and occasionally one of the pups may stray from, or fall out of, the nest. The female will usually be prompt in retrieving her offspring, either by picking it up with her mouth or by pushing it with her nose and forefeet. Should the female not notice the misplaced pup, you can try returning it to the nest yourself. If your gerbils are of the Mongolian variety, as most pet gerbils are, the female is not likely to mind your handling the animal. Note, however, that females of other, less common species may refuse to accept a pup after you've touched it, perhaps even killing it outright.

Before several more days have passed, the incisor teeth will have arrived, and the pups will be noticeably more agile. At this stage of development, you can safely handle the animals without disturbing the mother.

Shortly after the two-week mark has been reached, young animals should begin eating solid foods. You can give them fresh greens, unsweetened breakfast cereal, wholemeal bread, biscuit crumbs, milk, perhaps even some moistened puppy food. If one or two of the youngsters seem to have difficulty making the adjustment to solid food, try to coax them as best you can, for it will soon be time to wean them.

Weaning: You may get the notion that the pups are still too frail to wean as the three-week mark arrives. This is not so, as the animals are hardier

Females will usually be prompt in retrieving inquisitive pups that have strayed from the nest. They will do so either by picking them up with their mouths, or by pushing them back to the nest with their noses and forefeet.

than you think. You'll notice, in fact, that by now most or all of them are already exhibiting "adult" behavior climbing the cage, jumping to and fro, taking nourishment for themselves from the water bottle. For reasons mentioned earlier in this chapter, there's no getting around the fact that the transition must be completed before a second litter arrives.

After weaning, young gerbils may initially be housed in the same cage, but you'll have to separate the sexes before the end of the eighth week; otherwise, inbreeding will occur. Remember that the animals become sexually mature as early as nine weeks of age.

Around the fifth or sixth day the pups will be covered with a light mantle of fur.

Between the tenth and the twelfth day the pups' eyes will open.

A nest with healthy pups.

Understanding Gerbils

The Educated Observer

The better you understand your gerbils' habits and motivations, the more you will appreciate them. As an educated observer, you'll also be in a better position to anticipate and correct health or other problems that may arise from time to time. All of this makes for healthier, happier, and thus more interesting and responsive pets, thereby enhancing your enjoyment of them. Such a cycle is most desirable, for it is in the best interest of all concerned.

Despite the fact that the gerbils you have purchased were bred in captivity, their habits and their behavior will to a large extent be identical to those of their counterparts in the wild. There are exceptions, of course, most of which are linked to restrictions imposed by the size and makeup of their controlled environment.

Two other factors must also be taken into account. First, some gerbil behavior is not fully understood—either in the wild, or in captivity. Although certain observed behaviors may inspire simple, typically anthropomorphic theories among pet owners, some of which may actually approach the truth, the perceptive handler will realize that more complex (or sometimes less complex) motivations may be involved than the ones suggested by untrained and/or less than impartial observers. Indeed, some aspects of animal behavior may never be completely understood, and perhaps this contributes in some way to our unending fascination with the animals around us.

The other factor to keep in mind is that each animal is, to a certain extent, an individual and so may exhibit behavior that defies or surpasses what is considered the norm. Generalizations demand a stereotyping that ignores the exceptional in favor of the average. As such, they are valuable only insofar as they provide us with a reliable starting point— a basis for understanding.

Habits and Behavior

Preceding chapters have touched on virtually every aspect of gerbil behavior, but a few topics bear additional comment.

Scratching and Burrowing

Burrowing: In the wild, gerbils spend a lot of their time excavating (or renovating) their burrows. They are very well equipped for this activity, and they seem to enjoy it, so it's only natural to expect that your captive pets will regularly take on the task of digging up the floor dressing in their cage. How elaborate their excavations will be depends on the type and the quantity of floor dressing that is used.

A gerbil's burrowing is rather amusing to observe. Supporting itself on its hind legs, the animal leans forward slightly, then speedily begins flailing away at the target with its forefeet and claws. If the material it is displacing is sufficiently manageable, the animal will make quick progress, in spite of having to pause at regular intervals to kick away the collected piles with its powerful hind legs.

HOW-TO:
Understanding Gerbil Language

Gerbils communicate with one another in a variety of ways; almost all of which can be understood by the interested observer.

Vocalization

As quiet as the animals generally are, it is known that they are capable of certain vocalizations, which they are likely to utter under various circumstances. Newborns, for instance, squeak when they are hungry—which seems to be most of the time—or simply to announce their presence to the world, as all newborns are wont to do. Even as they graduate to what may be described as their juvenile and adolescent stages of development, young gerbils vocalize frequently as they play and socialize with their peers. By the time they are full-fledged adults, however, this behavior subsides considerably. Adults limit their squeaking primarily to moments of sexual agitation and to aggressive situations when a fight may be imminent. They also seem to "chat" sometimes when engaged in bouts of self-grooming.

It should be noted that the squeaking sound gerbils make (some liken it to the chirping of birds) is in no way bothersome to the human ear. The sound is so faint, in fact, that you have to be fairly close to the cage to hear it. Interestingly, tests conducted with sophisticated audio equipment have suggested that gerbils have a much wider repertoire of vocal sounds; unfortunately, however, these are beyond the range of human hearing. The significance of these sounds is still not understood. What we do know for certain is that gerbils have an advanced sense of hearing that is capable of detecting even low-frequency sounds.

Thumping

Gerbils also make an important nonvocal sound—that is, the rhythmic thumping of the hind legs that males typically display during courtship. Believed to be a manifestation of excitement, this behavior may also occur when an animal is placed in a new and unfamiliar environment. In the wild, such thumping serves its most useful communication function—signaling danger to other members of the colony. Sometimes other gerbils in the vicinity will duplicate the effort, in effect relaying a warning message before scurrying for cover into the relative safety of their burrows.

Gerbils are capable of this "feat" from around weaning age (three and one half to four weeks), and they accomplish it by drumming their hind feet, in unison, as they balance themselves with their tails. The

The rythmic thumping of the hind legs by the male is a typical display during courtship.

sound is more peculiar than disturbing, and you may find yourself impressed that such a tiny creature is responsible for it. As a warning device, it has been likened to the beaver's slapping of its tail, although the actual drumming action is more similar to the kind observed in rabbits

Body Language

Some moods and intentions are effectively communicated through body language. For example, you are already aware that gerbils often sit up on their hind legs. If, while doing so, they appear unusually stiff, with their paws clenched tightly in front of their chests, this is a sign of stress. In the wild, it would be more accurate to refer to it as the animals' "fight or flight" posture, meaning that they are prepared for either action,

Nonverbal communication among gerbils is also conducted through odor.

depending on the nature of the stimulus that triggered the response. On the other hand, when the stiff posture and clenched paws are not evident, animals that sit on their haunches are probably simply indulging in idle observation—a common manifestation of their natural inquisitiveness.

Curiosity, as you know, is a prime motivator among gerbils. That's why they'll usually perk up and, in effect, greet you, when you approach their cage, especially if you've just come home and they've been alone for a while. No doubt they're also well aware that yours is the hand that offers food, toys, and other pleasures, so their motivation in welcoming you is not strictly social; but here too, it may be argued, is a sign of their inquisitiveness—what did you bring this time?

At times, their curiosity borders on fearlessness, but do not be impressed. The fact is that captive-bred gerbils are not

Gerbils often sit up on their hind legs for various reasons.

aware of the dangers that exist in the outside world. Their lives, literally and figuratively, are sheltered ones. A gerbil that escapes from its handler, for instance, may think nothing of crossing the path of an unrestrained cat (if it survives the encounter, however, it will think twice next time).

Scenting

Nonverbal communication among gerbils is also conducted through odor. Utilizing the scent gland on his stomach (look for a bald spot), an adult male is able to leave an invisible mark on objects of his choosing. He does this by simply rubbing the gland against the object. Although the human nose is incapable of detecting the scent, gerbils, having a highly developed sense of smell, will notice it right away.

As mentioned earlier (page 16), scent also plays an important role in enabling gerbils to recognize and accept each other.

A father gerbil playing with one of his pups. Male gerbils take much interest in their family: They wash the babies, keep them warm and help rearrange the nest.

Burrowing and scratching are purely instinctive actions.

Scratching: Gerbils scratch at objects and obstacles even when they're not burrowing; if they're not trying to pry something open or to see what's behind it, then they are probably just sharpening (and shortening) their claws. Effective little tools, gerbil claws can easily shred cardboard and cloth.

Usually the amount of noise emitted during burrowing and scratching activity is minimal, but it varies, depending on the kind of floor dressing and, to a certain extent, the type of cage. You might assume, for example, that because you have an aquarium, any noise made by such a small animal would be muffled inside the enclosure's four walls. This is not necessarily so; if the floor dressing consists of dirt or sand (perhaps with particles of stone mixed in), you may be distracted by a small riot now and then. That is one reason why many owners prefer soft floor dressings.

Forget the notion that burrowing and scratching represent a latent or an active desire to escape captivity. These actions are purely instinctive. Certainly for captive-bred animals, their cage is their home. You will in fact notice, after the animals have grown used to you and you begin letting them

out of the cage for exercise, that some will return to it of their own volition, if it is accessible. You'll still have an occasional wanderer if you're not watchful, but more often than not the animal will reappear, when it is ready, with or without edible inducements.

There's another potential situation you should be aware of. Some day you may look into the cage and see that one of your pets is missing. Before you launch a panic-stricken search of your home, investigate whether the animal has simply buried itself under the floor dressing—there's a good chance that's where you'll find it. Usually a light rapping against the cage is enough to arouse the hiding (or sleeping) animal's curiosity, and it will pop its head up to see what the commotion is all about.

Playing and Fighting

These behaviors have been discussed in preceding chapters, but not in relation to one another. There is a connection, and knowing about it will help you to better understand some of your pets' actions.

It's clear that gerbils love to play—even the adults, though they don't display this behavior nearly as often as their offspring do. Pups, as you can imagine, play a lot, chasing each other around the cage, climbing and tumbling over one another while they explore their physical abilities and the limits of their environment. Even adolescent gerbils get into the act, but their games are more likely to consist of wrestling and shoving matches. More than simple exercise, these often become tests of strength—and of dominance.

When that happens, especially where adolescents or adults are concerned, the result can sometimes be violence—in other words, play-fighting turns to real fighting. If there is any consolation, it is that this is a rare occurrence, and even when it happens, there's an even chance that the disturbance will be settled quickly, with minimal damage. If a genuine brawl does ensue, it will probably happen when no one is around, so your involvement won't even begin until the fighting is over.

If, however, you are a pet owner who spends a fair amount of time observing the animals under your care, you will have plenty of opportunities to witness them at play. That being the case, there are several behaviors that should alert you that acts of aggression may be forthcoming.

The first of these is "boxing" with the forepaws. Though gerbils exhibit this behavior in play-fighting, it is also evident during genuine confrontations. Unfortunately, it is difficult to tell these situations apart. One clue may be the animals' tails, which are normally limp and lifeless. If they bend upward strongly, displaying forcefulness and determination, this may mean that the playing is getting out of hand.

Another sign of trouble is reciprocal pushing while the animals' heads remain locked in a face-to-face position. Here the scuffle is already under way, and more serious actions are

Gerbils like to establish property lines by skimming (crawling low while rubbing its stomach against a surface) along to mark their territory.

likely to follow unless you separate the brawlers or manage to distract them.

Grooming

Gerbils like to be clean, and they may spend several hours a day grooming themselves and/or their cage mates. This activity is most welcome because, in addition to promoting cleanliness, it stimulates the skin, keeps the coat shiny, and helps prevent fur from matting—all that, and no work on your part!

Because of their suppleness and agility, gerbils can reach most parts of their bodies with their tongues and teeth. For other areas, such as the face, neck, and ears, the animal uses a combination of tongue and forepaw, much like a cat.

Fighting does not always occur when two gerbils are introduced. With a little luck—and after a thorough sniffing of each other—the animals may accept each other from the start.

Being sociable animals (and because their cage mates are sure to reciprocate), gerbils enjoy grooming each other, especially when they're on the receiving end. You may chuckle when you see the tranquillity and trustful surrender their faces and bodies express while cage mates perform this service.

When one gerbil "burrows" underneath another and rolls onto its back, at the same time pressing its nose beneath its partner's snout, this is an invitation to mutual grooming. Gerbils that approach each other may sometimes engage in a reciprocal licking of the side of the mouth, but this is believed to be a form of greeting, not a grooming activity.

One thing a gerbil owner can do to help the animals be well groomed is to make sure that they are not exposed to high levels of humidity. A gerbil's skin produces oils—a byproduct of desert evolution—that serve to prevent excessive dryness. High humidity, however, counteracts the process, the

result being a constantly ruffled coat. Your pets will try to correct such a situation themselves by rolling in the floor dressing, or you might try giving them a sand bath (see page 27).

Sleeping

Gerbils are very active when they're awake, and the reason they can maintain such an energetic pace is that they rest or sleep frequently throughout the day. Sometimes, their sleep is so deep you may wonder whether they have all expired!

Often, the signs that a gerbil is about to take a nap are unmistakable, and somewhat charming. It will stretch out on its forefeet and lean into them, much like a dog or cat, after which a yawn usually follows. Gradually, the animal will assume one of its favorite sleeping positions—curled on its side, or lying on its stomach or even its back. In colder weather, gerbils tend to curl up into a ball when they sleep; whenever possible, they like to huddle close to their cage mates.

Gerbils really need their brief naps. Allow them to sleep undisturbed, and you will enjoy their waking hours all the more!

Gerbils may spend several hours a day grooming and cleaning themselves. In addition to promoting good health, this activity stimulates the skin, keeps the coat shiny, and helps prevent fur from matting.

Index

Perfect for Pet Owners!

PET OWNER'S MANUALS

Over 50 illustrations per book (20 or more color photos), 72–80 pp., paperback.

ABYSSINIAN CATS (2864-3)
AFRICAN GRAY PARROTS (3773-1)
AMAZON PARROTS (4035-X)
BANTAMS (3687-5)
BEAGLES (9017-9)
BEEKEEPING (4089-9)
BOSTON TERRIERS (1696-3)
BOXERS (9590-1)
CANARIES (4611-0)
CATS (4442-8)
CHINCHILLAS (4037-6)
CHOW-CHOWS (3952-1)
CICHLIDS (4597-1)
COCKATIELS (4610-2)
COCKER SPANIELS (1478-2)
COCKATOOS (4159-3)
COLLIES (1875-3)
CONURES (4880-6)
DACHSHUNDS (1843-5)
DALMATIANS (4605-6)
DISCUS FISH (4669-2)
DOBERMAN PINSCHERS (9015-2)
DOGS (4822-9)
DOVES (1855-9)
DWARF RABBITS (1352-2)
ENGLISH SPRINGER SPANIELS (1778-1)
FEEDING AND SHELTERING BACKYARD
  BIRDS (4252-2)
FEEDING AND SHELTERING EUROPEAN
  BIRDS (2858-9)
FERRETS (9021-7)
GERBILS (9020-9)
GERMAN SHEPHERDS (2982-8)
GOLDEN RETRIEVERS (9019-5)
GOLDFISH (9016-0)
GOULDIAN FINCHES (4523-8)
GREAT DANES (1418-9)
GUINEA PIGS (4612-9)
GUPPIES, MOLLIES, AND PLATTIES (1497-9)
HAMSTERS (4439-8)
HEDGEHOGS (1141-4)
IRISH SETTERS (4663-3)
KEESHONDEN (1560-6)
KILLIFISH (4475-4)
LABRADOR RETRIEVERS (9018-7)
LHASA APSOS (3950-5)
LIZARDS IN THE TERRARIUM (3925-4)
LONGHAIRED CATS (2803-1)

LONG-TAILED PARAKEETS (1351-4)
LORIES AND LORIKEETS (1567-3)
LOVEBIRDS (9014-4)
MACAWS (4768-0)
MICE (2921-6)
MUTTS (4126-7)
MYNAHS (3688-3)
PARAKEETS (4437-1)
PARROTS (4823-7)
PERSIAN CATS (4405-3)
PIGEONS (4044-9)
POMERANIANS (4670-6)
PONIES (2856-2)
POODLES (2812-0)
POT BELLIES AND OTHER MINIATURE PIGS
  (1356-5)
PUGS (1824-9)
RABBITS (4440-1)
RATS (4535-1)
ROTTWEILERS (4483-5)
SCHNAUZERS (3949-1)
SCOTTISH FOLD CATS (4999-3)
SHAR-PEI (4334-2)
SHEEP (4091-0)
SHETLAND SHEEPDOGS (4264-6)
SHIH TZUS (4524-6)
SIAMESE CATS (4764-8)
SIBERIAN HUSKIES (4265-4)
SMALL DOGS (1951-2)
SNAKES (2813-9)
SPANIELS (2424-9)
TROPICAL FISH (4700-1)
TURTLES (4702-8)
WEST HIGHLAND WHITE TERRIERS (1950-4)
YORKSHIRE TERRIERS (4406-1)
ZEBRA FINCHES (3497-X)

NEW PET HANDBOOKS

Detailed, illustrated profiles (40–60 color photos), 144 pp., paperback.

NEW AQUARIUM FISH HANDBOOK (3682-4)
NEW AUSTRALIAN PARAKEET
  HANDBOOK (4739-7)
NEW BIRD HANDBOOK (4157-7)
NEW CANARY HANDBOOK (4879-2)
NEW CAT HANDBOOK (2922-4)
NEW COCKATIEL HANDBOOK (4201-8)
NEW DOG HANDBOOK (2857-0)
NEW DUCK HANDBOOK (4088-0)
NEW FINCH HANDBOOK (2859-7)

NEW GOAT HANDBOOK (4090-2)
NEW PARAKEET HANDBOOK (2985-2)
NEW PARROT HANDBOOK (3729-4)
NEW RABBIT HANDBOOK (4202-6)
NEW SALTWATER AQUARIUM
  HANDBOOK (4482-7)
NEW SOFTBILL HANDBOOK (4075-9)
NEW TERRIER HANDBOOK (3951-3)

REFERENCE BOOKS

Comprehensive, lavishly illustrated references (60–300 color photos), 136–176 pp., hardcover & paperback.

AQUARIUM FISH (1350-6)
AQUARIUM FISH BREEDING (4474-6)
AQUARIUM FISH SURVIVAL MANUAL
  (9391-7)
AQUARIUM PLANTS MANUAL (1687-4)
BEFORE YOU BUY THAT PUPPY (1750-1)
BEST PET NAME BOOK EVER, THE
  (4258-1)
CARING FOR YOUR SICK CAT (1726-9)
CAT CARE MANUAL (1767-6)
CIVILIZING YOUR PUPPY (4953-5)
COMMUNICATING WITH YOUR DOG
  (4203-4)
COMPLETE BOOK OF BUDGERIGARS
  (6059-8)
COMPLETE BOOK OF CAT CARE (4613-7)
COMPLETE BOOK OF DOG CARE (4158-5)
DOG CARE MANUAL (9163-9)
FEEDING YOUR PET BIRD (1521-5)
GOLDFISH AND ORNAMENTAL CARP
  (9286-4)
GUIDE TO A WELL-BEHAVED CAT
  (1476-6)
GUIDE TO HOME PET GROOMING
  (4298-0)
HEALTHY CAT, HAPPY CAT (9136-1)
HEALTHY DOG, HAPPY DOG (1842-7)
HOP TO IT: A Guide to Training Your Pet
  Rabbit (4551-3)
HORSE CARE MANUAL (1133-3)
HOW TO TALK TO YOUR CAT (1749-8)
HOW TO TEACH YOUR OLD DOG
  NEW TRICKS (4544-0)
LABYRINTH FISH (5635-3)
NONVENOMOUS SNAKES (5632-9)
TROPICAL MARINE FISH
  SURVIVAL MANUAL (9372-0)

Barron's Educational Series, Inc. • 250 Wireless Blvd., Hauppauge, NY 11788
Call toll-free: 1-800-645-3476 • In Canada: Georgetown Book Warehouse
34 Armstrong Ave., Georgetown, Ont. L7G 4R9 • Call toll-free: 1-800-247-7160
ISBN prefix: 0-8120 • Order from your favorite book or pet store

(#62) R 3/96